THE COUNTRY DOCTOR'S YOUNGEST DAUGHTER

(A Memoir)

by

Frances Barnett Macdonald

with

Trish Macdonald Skillman

All photos from the Macdonald - Skillman Family Collection.
Stolen Owl Press logo design by Laura E. Bertrand
Photo page layouts and cover design by Jay Velgos

The OWL colophon is a trademark of Stolen Owl Press.

Published by Patricia Skillman - Stolen Owl Press
New Braunfels, TX 78130

For information on purchasing copies of this book or others currently available please visit: trishs.pianobaraustin.org

ISBN 978-0-578-17666-6

Printed & Bound in the United States of America by
AlphaGraphics®, San Antonio, TX

FIRST EDITION 2016

Library of Congress Control Number: 2016956203

INTRODUCTION

As a manuscript librarian I understand the importance of creating written accounts for future generations. Much has been lost over the course of our lifetime, simply because no one took the time to preserve the memories of those no longer with us.

Contained in these pages then, is not a genealogy but the story of my life *as I remember it.*

Whenever possible, I've attempted to verify factual references. While I've tried to maintain a chronological order, some incidents are recounted within broader time frames. The stories about my parents and my siblings' early lives have been recreated from my memories of mealtime conversations and family discussions through the years.

No life is either consistently joyful or free from sorrow. Mine is no exception. Some of the episodes that follow proved painful to write. Most reflect my overall outlook that life is what you make it and that how you react to a given situation is more important than weeping over that which can not be changed or controlled.

At eighty-eight I do not claim to have total recall. Others might remember or interpret certain situations differently, but what follows are *my* memories. I believe they are important enough to preserve. I hope after reading them that you agree.

September 1999   Frances Barnett Macdonald
Wichita Falls, Texas

For my great-granddaughter

RaBecca Michelle Bartee

Memories echo forever in the faces of each generation.

And

In Memory of Jay Velgos

1/16/1966 - 3/12/2016

Deeply missed, but never forgotten.

*Life is not a journey to the grave with the intention of
arriving safely in a well preserved body.*

*But rather to skid in sideways,
chocolate in one hand, wine in the other,
totally worn out . . . . .*

Screaming WOOO HOOO, what a Ride!!!

FOREWORD

Mother completed this memoir in September of 1999. Despite diminishing eyesight due to Macular Degeneration, she'd done this on a portable electric typewriter. Handwritten corrections dotted the manuscript.

It would be several years before her tech savvy grandson Jeffrey managed to scan the pages into a computer for editing. Eventually he and I interpreted the resulting mix of typed text and what the machine had read as hieroglyphic-like symbols.

Mother was a good writer. The memories and words are her's alone. At her request I did minor editing, suggesting alternate verbs or adjectives in a few places and varying sentence structures to avoid repetitions. In other spots I added notes from internet searches that corrected or clarified facts or knowledge that was not available to her at the time.

Fall 2015   Trish Macdonald Skillman
New Braunfels, Texas

Publication of this book would not have been possible without the love and assistance of the following family members:

Pamela Skillman Bartee for genealogical and research data.

Jeffrey Skillman for technical expertise, proofreading skills and extreme patience and support for his often stressed out mother.

Jay Velgos for invaluable technical and editorial suggestions, photo layout, and cover design.

RaBecca Michelle Bartee for continuing her great-grandmother's legacy.

November 18, 1942

Colin was about to go where a military wife could not follow. In two days I would be on a train, leaving the little Florida apartment to return home to Indiana, home to Mom and Dad to await the birth of our child.

That night, every time I closed my eyes, I kept hearing my father's voice calling out my nickname, "Bill William. Bill William." I sat up in bed and looked at the clock. It was about five A.M., but it was still dark outside.

The phenomena continued inside my head as I went out into the courtyard and began walking. Suddenly the voice stopped calling me. At that precise moment somewhere in one of the trees, a bird began singing the most beautiful song I'd ever heard.

With a heavy heart, I returned to my room. Somehow I understood that, although I would always be the country doctor's youngest daughter, my father's life was over.

CONTENTS

ONE

MY PARENTS' EARLY LIVES

Daniel Emmett Barnett

The first Barnett to arrive in the New World was a fur trader from Nancy, France. He married twice and had sixteen children. Family legend holds that one of his descendants married the granddaughter of Pocahontas.

(Note: A genealogical DNA test on the great-granddaughter of Frances Barnett Macdonald seems to discount this legend, which is also prevalent in histories of other Barnett lines. Her family now believes the relationship may be to a brother or other relation of John Rolfe, the Englishman who married Pocahontas.)

Whether or not this legend is true, there *are* physical signs that at least one ancestor from this branch of our family infused our lineage with that of a Native American, including my father's complexion and many of his facial features. Dad could not grow a beard and had very little facial or chest hair. My sister Lowene inherited his coloring and high cheek bones.

The Barnetts eventually moved from the East into Kentucky and then into Illinois where my father, Daniel Emmett Barnett, was born in 1875, the second child of Robert Barnett, a farmer, and Mary Elizabeth Martin. An older brother, Bruce, died at age two, but younger siblings, Ella and Ray, survived to adulthood.

Although my grandmother was still living when I was a child, she never talked about her family. I do remember being told that three Martin sisters married three Barnett brothers and I suspect that was correct, because I also remember Dad talking about a "double cousin."

Aunt Nan's Menagerie

In my father's day, family helped family as well as their neighbors. Great-Aunt Nancy Barnett and her husband owned a farm, but were getting up in years. One day my grandfather decided that Dad and Uncle Ray should go with him to do some repair work on the property. Dad, who was about thirteen, had been there before, but his younger brother had not.

Uncle Ray was fastidious in looks and action and did not like farming. He hated dirty work and dirty places. Even in work clothes he looked as if he'd stepped out of a fashion magazine.

As a farm wife, it was Great-Aunt Nan's duty to see to the care of the animals. Since a brood of baby chicks had hatched before warm weather, she'd made a place for them in her kitchen near the wood-burning stove. Also in makeshift pens in the kitchen, being bottle fed by Nan, were a baby pig, the runt from the litter of a sow who'd given birth to more babies than she could feed, and a lamb whose mother had died.

Nan was a fabulous cook. Dad had eaten meals at the farm before, but Uncle Ray had not. When he came in from his hard farm labor to wash up at the sink, he saw all the animals and whispered to Dad, "I can't eat here." Dad whispered back, "It's not dirt. It's just clutter. Don't insult Aunt Nan."

Still unconvinced, Uncle Ray sat down. When they began passing Aunt Nan's wonderful fried chicken, mashed potatoes and gravy, and six-inch-high yeast biscuits, he promptly forgot the animals and ate like the starving young boy that he was.

The Pie Thieves

A custom of the family's church was to sometimes surprise a member with a birthday party, honoring different members in different years, to keep the festivities secret. My Dad was sixteen the year his mother was chosen.

Hoping to distract my grandmother from the real reason guests would be coming to the house, Grandfather told her he had asked two men to help him with a farm project and had invited their wives to join them for the noon meal so the women could visit while the men worked.

Because the congregation's birthday surprise would include overflowing baskets of food, Grandfather suggested to Grandmother that she plan a simple meal and serve pie for desert. The next morning, not suspecting a thing, Grandmother began preparing the meal and put the two pies she'd baked on a window sill to cool.

The aroma of those fresh-baked goodies wafting on the breeze as the morning wore on convinced Grandfather that he and his sons deserved a reward for keeping their secret so well.

Around ten, Grandmother discovered that one of her pies was missing and immediately deduced what had happened. As she scolded the three guilty culprits, she glanced out the window, saw the caravan of buggies coming down the lane, and realized what was going on. End of lecture.

Dad Turns the Table

Before modern medicines and vaccines, epidemics of such diseases as diphtheria and typhoid and small pox caused many deaths. Grandmother Barnett devised her own form of preventive treatment to ward off diphtheria. She would roll up a piece of paper, insert some sort of awful tasting powder, and then blow it down each child's throat.

Once, knowing what was coming, Dad volunteered to endure the process before his siblings. Just as Grandmother was ready to blow, Dad blew first. End of treatment.

Leaving the Farm

Not all fatal illnesses in the 1800s were transmitted between humans. Grandfather Robert Barnett died after being bitten by a mad calf. Little was known about hydrophobia (rabies) back then and no serum existed at the time.

After her husband's death, Grandmother Barnett hired a manager for the farm and moved to town (probably to Sidell or Champaign) to run a hotel. During this time Dad completed his first year at the University of Michigan in Ann Arbor and Aunt Ella earned her teaching credentials and married. I'm sure Dad's decision to pursue a medical career was the direct result of the manner of my grandfather's death.

In those days, medical students completed both their university and med school courses after only four years of intense academic study. Internships in a rotation of specialties were served at a variety of institutions during summer breaks. Of course, a lack of funds often stretched academic years over additional calendar years. To supplement what little his mother could provide, Dad would complete a semester or two of college, then work a variety of jobs until he'd saved enough money to be able to return to school.

One position he held was as a Detroit street car conductor. Uncle Ray worked the same route as a motorman. The brothers' day was spent traveling back and forth from downtown Detroit to the end of Woodward Avenue.

Dad tried other things as well, but as soon as he had enough credits to obtain his credentials, he returned to Illinois to earn his college funds by teaching. He told many stories about his experiences during those times.

Acts of Kindness (and a Bit of Mischief)

At one school where Dad taught, part of the end-of-school festivities was a special presentation given by the students for their parents. One of Dad's young charges was supposed to recite a two-line poem, but by the time the poor child had memorized the second line, he would have forgotten the first.

Eventually the boy mastered his part. Or so he thought. When it came time for his part, Dad's pupil got through the first line okay, but couldn't remember the second. He peered into the audience and called, "I'm thinking, Mom. I'll get it in a bit." Finally, with a little prompting he managed to finish.

The next day the same student was working intently at his desk. Dad slipped up behind the boy and discovered that his seemingly slow pupil had drawn perfectly the vase of flowers sitting on Dad's desk. After school was dismissed, Dad took the picture to the boy's parents and the family took his advice to enroll their son in an art school.

Dad's former student eventually began his art career creating designs for a Chicago wallpaper company and went on to become well-known for his artistry.

Another of Dad's students came from a poor family that had no interest in sending their son to college. However, the boy was determined to continue his education. He'd earned enough to pay his tuition and to buy an overcoat (a necessity for chilly Midwestern winters), but lacked decent school clothing and the funds for books and housing, so he came to Dad for advice.

Dad didn't have much money himself, but he bought the boy two shirts and pants and gave him enough to pay for books and other incidentals. Then he helped his ambitious pupil find a place where he could live rent free in exchange for tending the building's furnace. Washing dishes in a family-owned café that Dad knew about provided the young man with two meals a day.

Another story from Dad's teaching days was of the Halloween evening a fellow teacher parked his buggy in front of the home of a young lady he was courting. While the teacher was visiting, some of his students unhitched his horse. Using a ramp they'd built, they pulled the buggy up on the flat-topped roof of a shed, coaxed the horse to follow and then re-hitched the rig.

Dad's co-worker came out to see, outlined by a full moon his poor horse and buggy. Thankfully, the mischievous students had left the ramp nearby, so the astonished teacher was able to retrieve his transportation and go home.

Dad's temporary teaching career provided fodder for many great stories. It also introduced him to my mother.

Cora Lucretia McGinnis

My Mother spoke little about her family or her early life. Most of what I learned was gleaned from an occasional casual remark. I do know that her family was Irish and had lived on the lands of a feudal lord during the time of Ireland's potato famine when many families, hoping for a better life, sought passage to America. Some had additional reasons to flee their country.

In order to feed his own and his neighbors' hungry families, Mother's Grandfather McGinnis killed one of the lord's deer. Unfortunately, he was arrested soon afterward. Poaching was considered a serious crime; the penalties were severe and starvation was not a valid defense.

With help from his grateful neighbors, my great-grandfather managed to escape. Paying for his passage by working as a member of a ship's crew, he came to America. Once here, he hired out as a farm hand and soon earned enough to buy his own land and send for his family.

The McGinnises eventually settled in Ohio. During the Civil War *my* grandfather, Lewis Abner McGinnis, ran away and enlisted in the Union Army at the age of sixteen. Although he fought in many battles, the closest he came to injury was when a Confederate bullet hit the canteen he wore across his heart.

After he returned from serving in the 82nd Ohio Regiment (with which his original company, the 61st Regiment Infantry Volunteers, had been combined), he married Lavenia Hoak and moved to Illinois. There my mother, Cora Lucretia McGinnis, was born in 1877. Her older siblings were Clyde and May. Lewis and Anna came along after her birth to complete the family.

Grandfather McGinnis was a Jack of all trades who farmed and taught school and held various positions in city government. Later in life, he invested in a tile factory that one of his son-in-laws built. As a hobby, he also raised two deer.

Mom Makes a Discovery

When Mother was not quite two, my great-grandfather Hoak, who had once been a newspaper editor, became ill. He'd been told that Mother, with her golden curls and blue eyes, resembled his late wife, so he asked Grandmother McGinnis to bring Mom back to Ohio so he could see her before he died. Mom sat on the old gentleman's lap jabbering away while he looked her over. When he fell asleep, she climbed down and went in search of her mother.

Hearing her mother's voice, Mom made a beeline for the kitchen, only to stop abruptly when she encountered Great-Grandfather's black cook and housekeeper. Until that moment, she had never seen a Negro, as African-American's were then called. The cook smiled and said, "Come on in, honey child, I won't hurt you," and soon Mom was chatting away once more.

A Young Girl's Life in the Late 1800s

Mother's family was fairly well-to-do, but by no means rich. This was reflected in their efforts to stretch every dollar, including those spent on teaching their daughters the refined graces of the time.

Mother had a lovely, though not very strong voice. Once when she was playing the piano - really just picking out the notes and singing, she told me that her parents had given her older sister May piano lessons with the intent that May would then instruct

7

Mother and Anna. But Aunt May made little effort to teach either of her younger sisters very much.

Another time, in answer to my question as to why she couldn't sew very well, I got the same response. May received the sewing lessons but did not pass them on. I knew this was because my grandparents didn't have the money to give all three girls individual lessons, but in my anger I couldn't understand why they hadn't given each one lessons in a different subject. Later I learned that Mother *had* been given elocution (or public speaking) lessons.

I once found a program for Mother's graduation and noted that she was listed as a soloist. When I asked her about it, Mom said that her number had been scheduled to follow a prominent soloist, a woman with a powerful voice. She said, "I was so embarrassed because, while I had a sweet little voice, that was all it was -- a sweet little voice."

Mother attended Normal School for two years, then passed a test to get her licence to teach. I once found a report card from a later test of a renewal of her teaching certificate. Her scores were above average in almost every subject.

Mother's career choice brought her much satisfaction and, although I never knew the details, it also brought her in contact with my father.

TWO

MY PARENTS' MARRIED LIFE
BEFORE I ARRIVED

Perhaps I simply never asked or was too young when the subject was discussed to pay much attention, but I don't remember Mother and Dad ever talking about where or when they were introduced. I do know their meeting was connected in some way to the fact that they both taught school, probably as a result of attending the same seminar or teaching conference. The marriage itself took place in Sidell, Illinois on June 12, 1901.

Regardless of how they got together, when Dad started the medical portion of his university training in Ann Arbor, he and Mother were already married. Because Uncle Ray began his law studies at the university around the same time, Grandmother Barnett had no one to help her run the hotel. So she gave that venture up and both she and Uncle Ray moved in with Mother and Dad. They rented a large house and put the hotel beds and linens and dishes to good use by renting their extra rooms to other medical students.

A year of Mother's credits from Normal School were accepted toward her pursuit of a university degree and she attended classes along with Dad. She had almost finished her second year when she became pregnant and was forced to give up her studies.

In the early 1900s, pregnant women did not flaunt their condition by appearing in public. Instead, they confined themselves to their homes and wore clothing designed to hide their expanding waistlines. Even the word pregnant was considered taboo in polite society. Thus, people would talk about a woman's confinement or delicate condition rather than her pregnancy. Thank goodness times have changed.

Bitter Disappointment

After my sister Love was born on August 10, 1902, Mother eventually returned to school. But at the end of her first semester back, she discovered she was expecting again. Mother was greatly upset by the situation, which in effect ended her quest for further education. I believe this is why Mother always resented my sister Lowene. Even much later when I became the fourth, and final, addition to our family, my beloved mother's lifelong dislike of her second child was still obvious.

To complicate matters, after her birth on February 19, 1904, Lowene was a sickly child. She had croup as a baby and, when she was a little older, pneumonia. For a while she was so ill she was delirious and kept talking about "kittles" on the wall. She was very upset that no one could understand what she was referring to. The medical students took turns rocking her to help Mom who was worn out from taking care of her ailing daughter.

Regardless of Mother's feelings toward Lowene, the medical students loved both little girls and often became baby sitters. Although these young men were supposed to be renting rooms only, Mother's and Grandmother's cooking so enticed them that soon they begged for evening meals, creating even more work to fill the hours Mother might have spent in class.

Earning a Degree

Mother wasn't the only one affected by becoming a parent. One of Dad's mathematics professors also had a family. Knowing Dad was also a father, this professor often asked Dad to care for his children - during class hours - when his wife had some commitment. Dad was forced to borrow notes from other students and take additional tests because of these extra-curricular duties. Luckily he excelled at math and easily passed.

Dad studied hard, but others in the class who knew this did not. They were constantly asking if they could copy his work. Dad always told them he didn't have the answers, but would then give a perfect recitation. Because of this and the fact that he was an older student, he earned the nickname Foxy Grandpa.

Perhaps as a result of being badgered to share his work, Dad wrote some kind of ethics code for the University of Michigan's medical school that was in use for many years. Although I don't remember the details of the code, I believe it addressed the attitude toward cheating on exams.

The Way Things Were

One of the institutions where Dad served his internship was Rush Hospital, a lying-in hospital in Chicago. (Lying-in was the term for what is now known as obstetrics and gynecology.) Besides additional training at the University of Michigan's hospital, he also learned all that was known at the time about disorders of the mind by interning at a mental institution.

Many of the mental wards housed patients in a catatonic state, which is characterized by the inability to voluntarily move your limbs. Dad became angry when he discovered that, for amusement, some of the interns from other universities were putting patients in odd positions. He began following after them and rearranging the patients's bodies in more relaxed positions. I know he would be pleased by how much attitudes toward those with mental illness have improved since he attended med school.

Establishing a Practice

After Dad graduated and received his medical degree, he practiced in Ludington, Michigan. One of his fellow students, the son of the local doctor, had no desire to return to his hometown and had told Dad about the position. Dad applied and was accepted. At this point Grandmother Barnett decided to return to Illinois to live with Aunt Ella and her family.

Because Ludington is on the eastern shore of Lake Michigan, the area was subject to severe winter weather. Being new on the job, Dad did not make much money. The old house where he and Mother and my sisters lived was cold and drafty.

Then, about eighteen months after Dad began his practice, his former classmate decided to return home and go into partnership with his father. Dad always believed this was because the son had not fared well on his own.

Since there was not enough business in Ludington for three doctors, Dad used the American Medical Journal to locate an opening in rural Missouri in what he always referred to as the Champ Clark area.

Modern maps make no reference to such an area, but I believe he was referring to the (then) sparsely populated country surrounding the little town of New Hartford in Pike County, Missouri. Pike County was home to U.S. Congressman and Speaker of the House, Champ Clark (1850-1921). Strengthening my assumption is a family genealogy that lists my brother Arthur's November 5, 1906 birthplace as New Hartford.

In any case, Dad helped Mother pack most of their belongings, then went on ahead to Missouri, leaving her to close up the house and follow with Love and Lowene.

Mother and the girls began their journey by boat from Ludington to Sheboygan, Wisconsin. All three became seasick during the choppy Lake Michigan crossing and were very glad when they docked and were on dry land once again. From Sheboygan, they rode the train to Illinois where Grandmother Barnett joined the family for the trip to their new home.

The Realities of Rural Medicine

There was so much illness in the early 1900s, especially in rural areas. People knew very little about sanitation and were drinking unboiled rain water that ran off the roofs where birds had nested. Dad had patients with diphtheria, typhoid fever, meningitis, scarlet fever and other bacterial viruses of the time. He saw such a variety of illnesses that he was soon able to recognize each one during its early stages. As a result, he was able to cure most patients fairly quickly.

One story he told was about a young girl who had boils. The treatment was an acid that was to be diluted in water and then taken orally. Unfortunately, while preparing the initial dose, the girl's mother accidently dripped some of the acid on her apron where it promptly burned a hole in the fabric.

Certain that even the diluted concoction would do the same thing to her daughter's stomach, the mother refused to administer the medication. Dad mixed some food coloring with pure water, added the acid, and sent the worried parent the *new* prescription. In no time, the girl was well.

Another time he told about an epidemic of lice in the schools. Dad helped the white families get rid of the lice and emphasized the importance of boiling bed linens to avoid recurrences. Mother was expecting my brother Arthur at the time and Dad had found a young black girl to take care of Love and Lowene. Mother caught the girl combing her own and then the girls' hair with the same comb.

Suddenly Dad had to cure an infestation of lice in his own home. He promptly taught the teacher at the black school how to eliminate lice so she could instruct her students' families.

Battling the Raging River

There were no bridges over the tributary river near Dad's practice, so people had to cross at places cut into the high cliffs. When the Mississippi flooded, the smaller river also overflowed its banks, making such crossings precarious. Since home visits were a routine part of patient treatment, practicing medicine in the Champ Clark area often proved to be a challenge.

Dad owned several horses and used saddlebags to carry his medicines and instruments needed for the emergency operations he often had to perform. Once when the river overflowed its banks, Dad was called to a new patient's home. The horse waded into the stream, but lost its footing and they were swept down river where the banks rose high on both sides. Dad couldn't swim, so he hung on for dear life. Finally, after a harrowing trip, the horse regained its footing and found a place to exit the stream.

Once he got back home, Dad sent word to the patient to explain what had happened. Dad told the man that if he would describe his symptoms, Dad would prepare the medicine to treat them. But someone would have to come after it. As Dad put it, "There are only five people for whom I'd try to cross that river again, and they all live in my house (Mother, Love, Lowene, Arthur, and Grandmother Barnett.) The patient sent someone after the medicine and as soon as the river subsided, Dad crossed over to follow up on his treatment.

Fighting the Prejudice of the Time

As one of only two doctors in the area, Dad soon discovered that the other physician refused to administer to the black population. When Dad took his Hippocratic Oath, he swore to treat everyone, regardless of color or race; and he did.

Once when he visited an elderly black lady, the river rose very high in a short time and he was forced to wait in her home until it was passable once more. His patient told him if that happened to him on that side of the river again, he was to come to her home and she would see that he had a comfortable wait.

After one especially heavy rain, Dad took her up on the offer. In addition to a dry haven, he was served coffee and sandwiches on the woman's best dishes and then shown to a big rocking chair to wait out the storm. Later, when one of his white patients on that side of the river heard that he'd stayed in a black woman's home, she belatedly offered him a bed and food too.

My Brother's Sweet Tooth

By the time my brother was about two, he'd discovered that a couple of elderly ladies who lived two houses away made wonderful cookies. To keep him from harm, Mother had penned him in the yard, but Arthur squeezed under the gate and went looking for some of those cookies. Dad reinforced the gate and thought he had the problem solved. But Arthur quickly learned to climb to the top of the low fence and then roll to the ground.

Mother decided to punish him by tying one end of a rope around his waist and fastening the other end to a big tree in the backyard, keeping an eye on him to be sure he didn't become tangled. She soon realized what she'd intended as punishment had become something to play with. There stood a delighted Arthur, shaking the rope and calling out, "Get up, Prince Dave!" (Two of Dad's horses at the time were named Prince and Dave.)

Dad's Sense of Humor

Dad's white patients paid well, but sometimes the blacks who sought out his services had no money. Still, Dad never refused to treat any of them. Often his pay was in produce, such as roasting ears or a chicken.

Once he treated a young black boy who'd cut his toe while hoeing corn. Dad cleaned the wound, took a couple of stitches, bandaged the injury, and then gave the boy a clean sock to wear to help keep out the dirt. He dressed the toe every day for about ten days and was ready to release his young patient when the boy asked, "How's it doing, Doc?"

Dad, ever the tease, removed the bandage but said, "Oh, I don't know, I may have to remove your toe." The young man leaped up and ran off as fast as he could. A few days later he came back with a big grin and handed Dad a few dollars.

Another time, Lowene announced that she wanted a black baby sister. When one of the black mothers brought her baby for a check up, Dad explained about his younger daughter's strange request and asked permission to take the baby to the house to show Lowene. The mother agreed, but went with him. Dad made Lowene sit on the floor then put the baby in her arms. A thrilled Lowene promptly asked, "Is it ours?" Dad had a little difficulty returning the baby to its anxious mother.

Time to Move on

When it was time for Love to start school, Dad looked at the local school system in the extremely rural area and decided he should move his family back up north where the educational system was more advanced. He hated to leave Missouri, for he loved the people and his practice had become quite lucrative. Still, he'd taught his patients good health habits such as boiling their water and drilling their wells away from animal waste, so epidemics were now much less common.

An American Medical Journal listing from a doctor in Rush County, Indiana who wanted to move to a larger city offered both a home and an office for sale. Dad visited the man and bought him out. To avoid a situation similar to the one in Ludington, their contract stipulated that the departing doctor would not practice in Rush County.

Once again the Barnett family packed up their belongings, shipped their household goods, and drove the horse and carriage to a new state. Grandmother Barnett, who'd decided to return to Illinois, was dropped off at Aunt Ella's on their way to Indiana.

The Little Town of Homer

Homer, Indiana, in Rush County's Walker Township, was a small town of approximately two to three hundred. Named for a Dr. Benjamin Rush, the county seemed a fitting place for a country doctor like my father.

A county road ran through the center of town. Northeast, seven or so miles as the crow flies, lay Rushville, Rush County's seat. Using the same measurement, about twelve miles southwest lay Shelbyville, the county seat of neighboring Shelby County. Of course, via the meandering county roads, the actual driving distances to both cities was almost doubled.

The town itself was laid out in a square, bisected by the main road and a railroad track and bordered on the west by a small stream known as Mud Creek. Two cross streets paralleled the creek at each end of town. To the south, another street ran parallel to the main road. Our house and my father's office sat about halfway down this block on the north side of the street.

As was only natural, some of the local people didn't want a new doctor, but dad soon became friends with most of them and his practice began to grow. Eventually he was ministering to people from as far as fifty miles away. Because patients who moved even further away continued to seek his services, he also found himself shipping prescriptions to Ohio, Michigan, Illinois, Kentucky, and even Canada.

Dad had a reputation as an excellent diagnostician. One surgeon told his colleagues, "When Dr. Barnett calls for a consultation, tells me the symptoms, and says he thinks the patient has such and such problem and needs my services, I get the operating room ready, for he seldom makes a mistake."

Dad's practice was thriving, but Mother was a very busy woman as well. She cared for her children, did the laundry and cooking, and sewed dresses for the girls. In addition, she kept Dad's books, acted as his secretary, and answered the phone.

Number Please

When Dad and Mother first came to Homer they were put on a telephone line with seven other families. This made it difficult to get the line to make calls to patients or to other doctors. Each home had a special ring and everyone knew which rings belonged to whom. Ours was two longs and two shorts. Whenever the doctor's phone rang, seven housewives listened in. So much for patient confidentiality!

Once Dad wanted to call another doctor for a consultation and found the line was busy. He continued to try off and on for an hour without success. Finally he listened to the conversation going on and discovered that all seven women were gossiping. Just then, one mentioned that she had a pot of beans on the stove. Dad broke in and said, "Madam, your beans are burning." Unfortunately, as she ran to check them, she dropped the receiver, so he was still unable to place his call.

When the woman returned, Dad asked politely if the ladies would relinquish the phone for him to make an emergency call. As soon as he rang the operator, he heard the sound of seven receivers being picked up again. He completed his call, but it was obvious that the doctor needed a private line. As it turned out, the operator was as bad as the housewives. A lawyer had to threaten the telephone company with a lawsuit if she listened in on any more business calls.

In order to get a private line Dad had to pay quite a bit extra. In fact, because different phone companies serviced different areas of his practice, he had to put in two separate lines in order to reach all his patients.

My Brother Learns a Painful Lesson

After returning to Illinois, Grandmother Barnett married a man named Miller. She and her new husband lived on a farm where they raised chickens and turkeys and kept bees for honey. Three-year-old Arthur had seen Grandmother use a broom to shoo the chickens out of the coop. Using the same technique, he found a stick and stirred up the bees with predictable and disastrous results.

Mother and Grandmother Miller removed over a hundred stingers from Arthur's body. They then spread a baking soda and water paste on the bites to soothe his itching, but the baking soda ran out before all the welts were covered. Grandfather Miller was dispatched to the neighbors for more. On the way, he met Dad, who'd been visiting someone in town. He applied castor oil to the bites. His smelly solution worked but Arthur was one uncomfortable little boy for some time and from then on, he was severely allergic to any kind of sting.

Dangerous Curiosity

Soon after Dad had moved to Homer he'd been elected county coroner. Although most of his duties involved accidental deaths, at least one murder occurred while he held the position. Until the trial began and he was called to testify, my father had custody of the gun that had been used in the killing.

After removing the bullets, he put the weapon on top of his tall dresser behind several other objects where he thought it couldn't be seen. However the mirror was tilted just right for his curious four-year-old to see the gun. Arthur climbed on a chair, got the weapon, and pretended to shoot everything in sight. When Mother came to see what he was up to, she became his next target.

Although she was sure Dad would have removed the bullets, Mother was still worried. She called Dad over from the office. He quickly confiscated the gun, locked it in his drug cabinet and gave Arthur a stern lecture on both the danger of firearms and on staying out of places he didn't belong.

With three active children around, my parents' lives were never dull. Things were, however, about to become even livelier.

Daniel E. Barnett,
probably his senior photo

Cora Lucretia McGinnis, age 22,
taken in 1899, possibly after
receiving her Normal School
credentials or first teaching job

Ray, Daniel, and Ella Barnett, with their mother Mary,
taken sometime after their father's 1896 death

Dr. Barnett's children in front of the Homer house, office at right.
Frances, Lowene, Arthur, and Love on porch, c. 1915-1918

Dr. D.E. and Mrs. Barnett's house in Homer,
office-pharmacy at right

THREE

AND FRANCES MAKES FOUR

On the morning of July 25, 1911, the population of Homer, Indiana increased by one when Dr. Wooden of Rushville delivered a third daughter to Dr. and Mrs. Daniel Barnett.

Shortly before I was due, Dad sent the girls to Illinois to visit Grandmother Miller and her husband. When they returned, all they could talk about was the red wagon they had as a surprise for their five-year-old brother. But Doc had his own surprise for them - a baby sister. Love was nine and Lowene was seven-and-a-half and I'm not sure that either girl considered me a very good trade for a red wagon.

Mother and Dad named me Frances Marie. Dad, who had really wanted another boy, promptly nicknamed me Bill William. The name stuck, since years later my nephews and niece grew up calling me Auntie Bill.

Because both Love and Lowene had been born in Michigan, Dad said they were wolverines (after the state's nickname.) He called Doc, who had been born in Missouri, a puke, although I never knew why. *(Note: A 2014 internet search explains the term which is now considered derogatory.)* Since I was born in Indiana, I was tagged a Hoosier.

Someone once said we four children must have been left on our parents' doorstep because none of us looked alike. Love had black hair, brown eyes and the coloring of a brunette. Lowene, whose complexion and features reflected our Indian blood, had wavy brown hair and gray eyes. Doc was very fair-skinned with the red-brown hair and blue eyes of our Irish ancestry. Then there was me - fair complexion, straight platinum hair, and changeable hazel eyes that picked up the color of whatever I was wearing.

Since Grandmother Miller was white-haired at sixteen, I have no doubt which side of the family I took after. Being what's known as a tow-head, I was constantly teased about my hair. As a small child, whenever I was asked what color it was, I would lisp, "It's 'phite', but 'ist' getting black."

Through the years my platinum hair turned ash blond, then golden blond, and finally the snow white I have now. Not once did the black hair I so longed for materialize.

The Bread Box Baby

When I was a baby and Mother had to go to the dentist or to Indianapolis to purchase clothes, she would leave me with Mr. and Mrs. Boots Abernathy, who ran a general store. Although they had none of their own, they loved children.

Mrs. Abernathy, who was also Homer's post mistress, was often busy waiting on mail patrons or helping her husband. To keep me out of trouble, she would convert the store's big wooden bread box, which was between four and six feet square, into a play pen. She stacked the wrapped bread on one of the counters, placed blankets in the bottom of the box, and in I'd go. If I was awake, she added some toys to keep me occupied.

The Pennsylvania train came through Homer and dropped off mail three times a day. Each family was assigned an individual box in a large wooden cabinet, which was open in the back to allow Mrs. Abernathy access, but glassed on the outside so people could see if they had any mail. Of course, it was my job to keep everyone who came in entertained. Old gentlemen played peek-a-boo and patty cake, and waved bye-bye.

Mother didn't have a bread box play pen, but she had discovered another solution to keep me out of trouble.

When Love had been very small she'd been frightened by a chicken that flew up into her face. Someone, probably my brother, decided it would be funny to scare me as well by tossing a bunch of feathers into *my* face. Soon after that incident, my family learned that they could keep me in one room simply by putting a single feather in each doorway.

Frances Gets Bored

Homer had three churches -- the Baptist, the Christian and the Christian Union. Mother was a Methodist and Dad belonged to the Disciples of Christ, so they joined the Christian church. Because she'd been a teacher, Mother was often asked to direct the church's annual Christmas program. One year she brought me with her to one of the rehearsals.

I sat quietly for about as long as any three-year-old could while the teenage performers recited and sang each part of the program over and over. Then, just as they were finishing up, I stood up, turned around and somersaulted over the pew I was in. That was so much fun, I kept going over the next and the next until I got to the last pew in the church. Watching my little white panties disappear and reappear as I flipped, the teenagers became tickled and broke up the song.

When Mom finally corralled me, the conversation went something like this:

"Don't you know how to behave?"

Not knowing what the word meant, I responded, "No."

"Then I won't bring you again."

"Fine."

New Shoes and a Short-lived Friendship

During those early years I had few girls my age to play with until Mother invited the Washburns to join us for Sunday dinner and I met their daughter Agnes.

Our minister rotated his duties, preaching one Sunday at the Christian Church and the next at the Christian Union. He also went to two other churches each evening. Because he spent so much time traveling, church members were expected to provide his noon meal. In theory, families took turns, but Mom had a reputation as a wonderful cook. Sometimes it seemed as if we had the minister as our guest more than our fair share of Sundays.

Since Dad often had to leave in the middle of meals due to some medical emergency, Mother began inviting other couples to join us on Sunday. Thus Agnes Washburn and I became good friends.

One Sunday Agnes and I spent the afternoon sliding down the cement bannisters on each side of the steps going up to our porch. As a result, I wore out the soles of my new Mary Janes. (Patent leather shoes with a strap across the top of the foot.) My provoked father told me I didn't deserve another new pair and would have to go barefoot to Sunday school..

All week I worried. Then late Saturday afternoon Dad took me to Rushville (the county seat and nearest big town) and bought me the ugliest pair of shoes imaginable. I didn't care what they looked like; I was just happy that I wouldn't have to go to church barefoot. I told my startled father, "Won't everybody be pleased and surprised to see Dr. Barnett's youngest daughter walk down the aisle wearing such beautiful new shoes?"

When I was six my friendship with Agnes ended abruptly.

Agnes had what her family assumed was a simple cold and sore throat, so they didn't bother to bring her to Dad to be examined. Unfortunately, my friend actually had spinal meningitis and within a short time she was gone. I attended her funeral but couldn't really reconcile the idea of Agnes being in heaven. For a long time after that, death frightened me.

I've often wondered what role that early episode might have played in the precognitive dreams I was to experience much later in life.

Puppy Love Lost

For some time after Agnes died, I had no one my own age to play with. Dad's solution to the problem was to add a puppy to our household.

Because the rabid calf that had bitten his father had gotten the disease from the bite of a large wild dog, Dad had always feared large dogs. He decided getting a small dog might help him get over this, so he bought a fox terrier which he allowed me to name. *Gladys* was just a puppy but *he* accompanied me everywhere, including the grocery store and the post office, where I had to leave him outside.

Some of the old-timers who sat on the benches in front of those buildings liked to tease Gladys. Because of this rough-housing, the puppy began jumping and nipping at me as well, tearing my stockings and clothes. As a result, Dad felt he had no choice but to place Gladys with a farmer who had other dogs.

The day after Gladys was exiled, Dad walked me to the post office. When the old men asked where my puppy was, Dad pointed to my torn socks and clothes. "Your idea of play made him too vicious," he told them. They all apologized, but the damage was already done. Once again I'd lost my playmate.

Party Behavior

I really don't remember it, but I have a photo of me holding Dad's hand and I was told that the picture was taken at my only birthday party. I appear to be about four or five.

However, I do remember attending someone else's party. Chairs had been lined up against the dining room wall, each in a special place. Two or three were close together and several girls were sitting in them chatting with one another. I was alone, so I scooted my chair over to join them. The mother came to the dining room and told me that my chair belonged against the wall and for me to put it back. I did what she instructed, then went back over and sat on the floor near the others.

Soon the mother came back into the room and told me to get up off the floor and act like a lady. I rose and thanked her for inviting me to the party and then went home. When I got there, Mother asked what kind of cake they had served and since I hadn't eaten any, I had to tell what happened.

Needless to say, although those same girls sometimes came to play at my house, I never again went to their's.

The Indian Encounter

Because my brother wanted to follow in our father's footsteps, people in Homer began calling him "Little Doc." Over time, the family shortened the nickname to simply Doc and this is how I think of him even now.

Doc often talked in his sleep and was also known to sleep walk. Once in awhile he stayed overnight with his friend, Wally Inlow whose parents were deaf. Because Mrs. Inlow's deafness had resulted from a childhood disease, she could say a few words, but Mr. Inlow had been deaf from birth and was mute.

One night before they went to bed, Doc and Wally read a story about Indians. The boys were asleep in the second floor bedroom, when Doc suddenly yelled out that Indians were looking in the window. Wally woke his parents and caused quite a commotion as they searched the house. When they realized Doc wasn't with them, the three Inlows rushed back upstairs only to find their overnight guest still blissfully sleeping, unaware his dreaming had triggered such panic.

The Realities of War Come to Homer

Despite my early fears of feathers and death, I was really rather brave as a child. During World War I, my sisters and their friends knitted socks for the soldiers overseas. One afternoon Loren Hodges, a friend of Doc's who lived across the street, decided to join them. Loren was knitting away when suddenly he ran the needle into his thumb. The other girls all fainted, but I calmly led Loren across the yard to Dad's office. After he treated Loren's wound, Dad tended to the swooning girls.

Death brought the reality of war close to home as well, since combat and the terrible influenza epidemic that raged during those years took a large toll on the young men from our county.

Mrs. Carr, who lived across the street, had two sons. Raymond, her favorite, became our first casualty when he died from the flu while overseas. His camp commander called my father to ask that Dad break the news to the family. I remember listening while Dad took down the information about when and where they would be bringing Raymond's body home. Everyone was solemn and upset and, once again, I became quite frightened.

When Dad went across the street to talk to Mr. and Mrs. Carr, Raymond's mother became so distraught that he was forced to give her a sedative. From that day forward she was an entirely different person.

Face to Face With an Epidemic

Eventually, some of the soldiers on leave brought the flu home with them. The disease spread so rapidly through our area that Dad had trouble keeping up with his patients. For three weeks he didn't go to bed at all. He simply came home to bathe and change clothes, then went out again.

There was little he could do, for there was no remedy. His simple treatment was complete bed rest, lots of liquids, aspirin for the ache, and nourishing but light meals.

Entire families came down with the flu. Healthy farmers helped feed and water the livestock for those who were suffering. After they themselves became ill and those previously afflicted had recovered, the favor was returned. As mothers got better they would help the children, who seemed to have lighter cases. When the most severe cases were at their crisis, Dad stayed with his patients. Because he'd had no sleep he would sit in a chair and doze, waking often to check on everyone.

One day as the epidemic wore on, Dad brought home two great big pieces of beef. He told mother to get out her biggest pots and start cooking. The children of two of the families he'd been treating were starving because their parents were too sick to care for them. He helped Mom peel potatoes, carrots, and onions, and when the meat was almost done he added the vegetables.

He took a pot to one family and fed the children himself. Then he gave some broth to the parents, put the leftovers in the ice box, washed the dishes, and left. At the second house, he repeated the process. Thanks to those meals both families survived. Indeed, despite many deaths in surrounding communities, I don't believe Dad lost even one patient.

Eventually our family caught the flu too, but we had fairly mild cases, perhaps because Dad put so much emphasis on good nutrition and we were otherwise quite healthy. Since none of us experienced the worse symptoms at the same time, one of us was always recovered enough to care for the next one who took it.

Once the epidemic died down, Dad came home and went to bed with his own case of the flu. Like most doctors, he was not a particularly good patient. Fortunately for us, after three weeks with little sleep, he slept most of the time and wasn't able to complain too much.

Relief at Last

When a false armistice to the war was declared shortly before the real one, Homer's children had a parade. Doc led our cow, which I rode while banging on a tin pan. We marched around the square that formed the little town of Homer singing "America" *(Note: It's unclear whether she's referring to "America the Beautiful", written prior to 1900, or Irving Berlin's "God Bless America", which was copyrighted during the last year of WWI.)*.

Soon after that, the real armistice was signed at the eleventh hour of the eleventh day of the eleventh month. What we then knew as Armistice Day is now celebrated as Veteran's Day to honor those who served or died in all wars.

A Family Member Shares His War Experiences

Mother's sister Anna had married a man of German or Austrian heritage whose family, like so many others, had changed their name upon arriving in America. Thus, the Von Tromps, not knowing the meaning of many English words, became the Tramps.

During the war, Anna's son Worth Tramp trained at Camp Knox (now Fort Knox) in Kentucky. One weekend Mother packed a lunch and Dad drove all of us down to take Worth to a park for a picnic. Worth was so hungry for a home-cooked meal he almost made himself ill feasting on Mother's fried chicken, potato salad, tomatoes and watermelon and cake.

After we finished eating, he described how the camp washed dishes. Using lukewarm water and very little detergent, they put all the utensils into a huge tub, stirred them around with a milking stool, and then left them to dry. He told us the tin plates were cleaned a little better, but not much.

Later, when Worth returned from overseas duty, he visited Homer and told us a bit about his experiences. While he was in the Argonne Forest, a German plane strafed the road he was traveling. Worth abandoned the ammunition truck he was driving and ran into the trees only moments before his vehicle was blown up. For two days he wandered around lost in no-man's land without food or water, dodging the enemy.

Eventually he came across a Red Cross camp and asked for something to eat. He was told that they had nothing to give him. At that moment someone passed by on the way to the officer's mess with a tray piled high with steaks. Apparently their shortages applied only to foot soldiers.

Worth continued on until he found a Salvation Army camp. There he received some stale donuts, a glass of milk and directions to his outfit, which had moved. While he was visiting, he told my mother, "Aunt Cora, don't you ever pass a Salvation Army bucket at Christmas without tossing in some money."

FOUR

SCHOOL DAYS

Although we would eventually complete our secondary educations elsewhere, all of us attended grade school in Homer. Love entered first grade in the old two-room school, but began second grade in the recently completed consolidated school that served the entire township. Lowene followed the next year.

A few months before his fifth birthday, Doc joined his older sisters. Because he'd heard Love and Lowene recite and had memorized their lessons, he quickly impressed his first grade teacher. But she soon discovered that, while he gave correct answers, he couldn't actually read. To prevent this from happening in another family, Dad notified the school board that classroom texts and lesson plans needed to be revised annually.

Dad as Tutor

Since he'd been a teacher, Dad knew the importance of study. The four of us gathered around the dining room table every evening to complete our homework by the light of a kerosene lamp. Dad supervised and provided help as needed. Sometimes when we were too slow responding, he would thump us on our heads with his forefinger -- a very annoying and painful habit.

Once when he thumped me, I dared to voice the opinion that I'd be able to think much better if he would abandon the practice.

A Schoolmate Misbehaves

When I was in the first grade, I developed a bad cold and missed a lot of school. After I returned to class, I was not allowed to go out for recess. Another student named Leondis also had to stay in. The substitute teacher we had at the time spent recess on the playground with the other students.

For a while, things were fine and I sat quietly studying. But then Leondis began chewing an old rubber band and snapping it at me, spraying me with saliva. It was disgusting and I asked him to stop. He didn't, so I got up and moved away. His next move was to chase me around the room.

In the midst of all this, a vase that belonged to our regular teacher was knocked off the desk and broken. Horrified, I began crying and ran outdoors without my coat.

My brother saw me and took me over to the substitute teacher. She scolded both of us, then made me sit in one corner and Leondis in another until school let out for the day.

I loved my regular teacher and was sure I'd broken an heirloom. That night I told Dad I wanted to buy her a new vase. When he explained the situation and offered to buy a replacement, the teacher laughed and told him not to bother because the vase had come from the dime store. Nevertheless, when Dad and I found an exact duplicate, I was very relieved.

Our Learning Environment

Our school in Homer was a ten-room brick building that housed the first through twelfth grades. Grades one through six were on the first floor, two grades to a room. The girls' and boys' toilets were in the basement, as was a sink with a pump where we could wash our hands. The basement was always cold and the toilets had metal seats and no flushing mechanism. Like outhouses, chemicals were added periodically to keep down the odor. Let me tell you, in that atmosphere, when nature called, students did not linger.

There was a drinking fountain on the first floor. Each classroom had its own cloak room for outer garments and shelves for lunch boxes. Since I lived nearby, I usually went home for lunch unless Mother was going to be away.

The upstairs held seventh and eighth grades in one room. Freshman and sophomores shared a classroom; juniors and seniors were assigned to another. Individual rooms for domestic science and industrial arts and a big auditorium where we studied and gave programs completed the second-story floor plan.

One such student program was a play called "The Blue Bird" which involved the entire school. Each class sang as a chorus and a few students, including several from my second grade class, played minor parts. To my embarrassment, I flubbed my one line, but the play itself was a huge success.

Homer's school was located on about three acres. A wooden fence with iron pipes threaded through wooden posts ran along the front of the building. Those pipes were a wonderful place to turn flip-flops. (You can tell that my behavior hadn't changed much since the pew flipping episode.)

Since little girls' panties showed as they somersaulted over the pipe, most mothers made bloomers (loose pants gathered above the knees) for them to wear under their dresses. My brother made a big fuss about *my* panties showing, so Mother, whose limited sewing skills didn't extend to making clothing, had a seamstress make me a few dresses with matching bloomers.

Children who lived in rural Walker Township were brought to school in a horse-driven school hack. I wanted to ride in the hack, so one of my friends, Lowene Edwards (who'd been delivered by my father and named after my sister), invited me to stay overnight and ride the hack again the next morning.

I found the experience very entertaining. We rode all over the township delivering the other kids to their homes. Everyone teased one another, sang songs and really enjoyed themselves. I was so jealous I told Lowene I wished I lived in the country. She assured me that sometimes it was boring. The school later switched to motorized buses, but I doubt they were ever as much fun as those horse-driven hacks.

Nature Provides a Lesson

At the top of our school building was a cupola (a small tower at the peak of a roof, much like a church steeple) where the school bell hung. One winter day the caretaker thought he saw something in the cupola. When he climbed up to investigate, he discovered an egret with a broken wing. The cupola was covered with ice and the caretaker slipped and fell, but he managed to hold on to the bird, which had apparently become lost from its flock on the way south and was too weak to fight.

We had no vet in our area, so the caretaker called Dad who treated the man's bruises and sprained ankle, then splinted the bird's wing. After that the avian patient was kept in a cage at the school and fed by older students until it was able to fly.

It was quite a treat for us to observe that species of egret, a member of the heron family which usually spent much of its time in more southernly states. The episode became a good lesson for all the classes. We learned about the bird's diet and habitat and even had a geography lesson.

Learning to Mind Dad

Once when I was about seven, I wanted to play with younger classmates who lived on the other side of Mud Creek. When I asked Dad if I could go, he said, "No, those girls' mother is very ill. I don't want her disturbed by three noisy children."

After Dad had gone to his office and I had completed my morning chores, I repeated my request to Mother. Not knowing that Dad had already said no, she gave me permission.

I took the girls way out to a tree in their orchard where we played house and lots of games. Suddenly I saw that my father, who was making his house calls, had arrived. I knew I was in trouble, so I said goodbye to my friends and quickly ran home.

Dad asked the nurse how long I'd been there and commented that he had forbidden me to visit. Both the mother and nurse immediately spoke up in my defense.

"Don't you dare punish that child," the nurse told him. "This is the first time this week this mother has had a few hours of peace and quiet. Her girls have been all over her and the bed."

Once I got home I crawled under my bed, but I was still in plain view to anyone entering the room. When my father returned, he told mom what had happened and found she'd given me permission to go. Dad then came to the bedroom, put his hands behind his back, and walked up and down beside my bed saying, "If I only knew where that little girl was, I would punish her. Then she would not run away or disobey ever again."

During his performance, I was too frightened and ashamed to speak, so after a while he went back to talk to Mother. By the time he returned, I'd cried myself to sleep. He had to lift the bed so he could pick me up and tuck me in. The next morning nothing further was said about my disobedience. But you can be sure that after that, I never ran away again; I always asked permission before I visited friends; and I learned to accept the word "no".

Grandfather Takes Offense

When I was in the fourth grade, my Grandfather and Grandmother McGinnis came from Iowa to visit us. My class had just begun to study American history and, as a Civil War veteran, Grandfather McGinnis avidly read anything he could find about that conflict, including fourth grade textbooks.

Unfortunately, the day my grandparents arrived, I had just received a dirty-worded note from a boy in my class who shall remain anonymous. I'd stuck the note into my history book because I wanted to show it to Dad. To my horror, Grandfather picked up the text to see what it said about *his* war.

I asked politely if I could have the book back for just a minute. When he refused my request, I grabbed the book and removed the note, then handed the book back to him.

Grandfather was furious and told my father how rude I had been. Dad broke off a peach tree limb and gave me the only whipping I ever had. Then, after Dad calmed down, he decided to ask for *my* version of the episode.

I explained that I didn't want Grandfather to have to read the note I'd slipped inside the book and assured him that I'd tried to make my request politely. Dad read the naughty note and promptly asked Grandfather about the finer points of our little confrontation. Grandfather had to admit that I had not become (what he considered) rude until he refused to let me see the text for a moment. I never knew what Dad said to him after that, but both he and my father later apologized to me.

Tag-along Sister

My brother and Loren Hodges, the boy across the street, disliked having me tag along after them. Then they discovered that I could run very fast. They paired me with another neighbor, Bobby Frow. He was my age, but I usually left him far behind in our races. The two older boys tried handicapping me by giving Bobby several yards head start, but I was still victorious.

Bobby, who hated to lose, began throwing corn cobs at Doc. The pair bombarded each other for a while until Bobby decided that chunks of coal made better weapons. Doc, who was five years older and could throw much better than Bobby, hurled a lump that cut Bobby over the eye. Of course, Dad was asked to clean and patch up the wound.

That time, Doc earned a session with the peach tree limb.

A Classmate Flaunts her Superiority

Indiana tested all fifth grade students annually. These tests were similar to those that are given even now to assess students' progress at various points during their educational career. Ours helped determine the quality of the texts we were using as well as compare the effectiveness of the teaching in the various schools. Results were made available to the parents, who could then make informed decisions about accelerating their child's education.

Based on her general scores, one of my fifth grade classmates was allowed to skip a full school year and advance to seventh grade. Because the grade she skipped included intense study in math and history, she continued to join our class for lessons in those subjects.

Nevertheless, she missed few opportunities to remind the rest of us that she had a superior intellect. Perhaps I was overly sensitive, but the taunts she directed at me seemed especially mean-spirited. Only during my college years, after a decade of privately questioning my own abilities, did I learn the truth about the situation. (I'll discuss this later in the book.)

Horse and Buggy Days

Because so many students were needed to plant and harvest crops in our rural area, Homer had only eight months of school. Dad sent Love, Lowene and Doc to Rushville for the extra month of the school year. To get there, they drove his horse and buggy.

Dad had also bought a five-gaited riding filly named Pet. Although he seldom found time to ride, both Love and Doc eagerly kept the horse exercised. Pet was very fast and hated for anything to pass her.

One day Love rode Pet out to visit her friend Mabel Hiner and stayed a little too long. Pet was tied to a hitching post and had eaten all the grass she could reach and was ready for her stall and her feed. As they rode along the road to the main highway, Love allowed three cars to go around them. On the highway itself still another car passed.

Pet decided she'd had enough and took off at full speed. Soon she was ahead of all four vehicles.

Love had beautiful long black hair. At the time, it was the style to wear *rats* in your hair over your ears. (Rats were mesh wiring or webbing worn under the hair and held on with hair pins. The resulting look resembled a page boy style.) By the time Pet's hooves clattered across the oak floor boards of the bridge over Mud Creek, the filly was really traveling. Hearing the commotion, we looked out to see my sister hanging on for dear life.

When Pet swerved into the alley that led to our barn, Love was no longer in the saddle, but was hanging to one side in mid-air. Pet slowed abruptly, then walked calmly into her stall. She waited docilely while we pulled a very limp Love, whose beautifully done hair was now quite straggly, from the horse's back. A few minutes later, Wally Inlow, whose home the pair had passed, carried in the hair pins and rats that had been lost on the way home.

FIVE

LIFE IN OUR LITTLE WORLD

Our house in Homer was rather small for a family of six. We had a parlor and a sitting room, which we'd probably call a family room these days, for we lived in that room. Originally, there were two bedrooms. Then a remodeling spree changed the kitchen into a third bedroom and the back porch into a kitchen with a large pantry. Six of us shared a single bathroom.

A central hall connected the bath, the original kitchen (or later bedroom) and the dining room. The stairs to the basement were between the former kitchen and the dining room. Also off the hallway was a big closet that was a catch-all for everything -- much like the closet in the Fibber McGee and Molly radio show.

(In this old comedy show, every time Fibber went to put in or take something out of that closet, his wife Molly would call out a warning. Fibber never listened, so as soon as he opened the door, things he'd previously crammed in came crashing down. Listeners loved the sound effects of this auditory punch line.)

Our catch-all closet held, for a very short time, two Ku Klux Klan robes. They disappeared soon after my father, who had been led to believe the organization was simply a patriotic group, discovered the Klan's true colors and demanded that his and mom's names be removed from the membership rolls.

All the Modern Conveniences

Our food was cooled in an icebox that held a hundred pounds of ice and someone had to be home on delivery day to let the iceman in. Later we got an electric refrigerator, although a very primitive version of today's appliance.

In winter we used a big base burner which took buckets of coal to keep going. At night the burner had to be banked to hold the fire until morning. Eventually we got a coal furnace that required less stoking, and even later, a more advanced model with an automatic stoker.

Although we had indoor plumbing, we pumped drinking water from a very deep well. A second pump in our basement drew water from a cistern. (A cistern was a large barrel-like underground container built of bricks. Rainwater seeped into the barrel from the saturated earth that surrounded the cistern.)

Because Dad had taught us to drink only pure water, we never drank from the cistern pump, but used that water for laundry which was boiled in a copper or aluminum tub with lye soap and stirred with a broom handle. Next each garment was put through a hand-cranked wringer to remove the soapy water.

Items were then rinsed in a tub of fresh water and wrung out again. Lye soap is harsh, so the procedure had to be repeated a second time before the clean laundry could be carried upstairs and hung on the outside line. In the winter, when it was too cold to dry things outside, we strung clothesline across the basement.

Once things dried, they had to be ironed. Before we got electricity, we had to heat a heavy, solid cast iron on the wood-burning stove, then hold it with a hot pad and use lots of elbow grease to smooth out all the wrinkles in the dampened fabric. Since the iron lost its effectiveness as it cooled down, a second and third iron were always heating on the stove. Two of the three were considered improved models because their handles could be detached and kept cool while the irons were heating.

Since I was the youngest, I usually ironed flat pieces such as handkerchiefs, tablecloths and napkins, and linen hand towels.

Mother kept a close watch to be sure I didn't burn myself. My sisters were responsible for their own clothing and Mother ironed her own and Dad's and Doc's things as well as the white dress shirts Dad wore every day. Wash day was a major event.

Gypsy Travelers

Roving bands of gypsies often traveled through Homer, usually in a caravan of ten or so wagons. We kids had heard tales of gypsies kidnaping little children. Whether these were true, I don't know, only that we believed what many adults had said.

Once when I was about five, Dad and Mother were away and Love was in charge when a caravan of highly decorated wagons crossed the bridge over Mud Creek. She and Lowene were sitting on the front porch and saw them approaching. I was at the end of our back alley playing. Lowene came running and brought me home. Love locked every door and we all crawled under the bed. Since Mother and Dad never locked our doors, they had a hard time getting into the house when they returned.

The gypsies usually stayed in town only long enough to purchase groceries at Swartz's store. They remained in the store a long time and usually stole candy or other small items while they were there. Some years after the above incident, I had gone to the grocery store when another band of gypsies came through.

Mr. Schwartz, the owner, was gone and his wife begged me to stay and watch the two women who came in. As she explained, "Usually one asks for something we keep at the back of the store and the other remains up front, stuffing items in her deep flowing sleeves."

Sure enough, one women asked for kerosene which was at the back of the store. While she and Mrs. Schwartz were gone, the other asked for first one item and then another and kept changing her mind. I did my best, but I know she stole some cookies and candy while I was getting a dozen eggs. Even so, Mrs. Schwartz was grateful that they didn't get more than that.

The Fire

When I was seven, Mother hired a young woman named Rosie, who was mentally slow, to help clean and baby sit as needed. One evening Rosie was supposed to be watching me. I'd been put to bed but woke up to see flames and smoke from my window. I called out, but Rosie, who was afraid of fire, had seen the same flames and run home to hide. I was alone.

Still wearing my nighty, I ran toward the fire. The blaze turned out to be in the ice cream parlor attached to Schwartz's store. The second floor of the store itself housed the Masonic and Redman lodges. The Manilla and Rushville fire departments had been called, but neither had arrived, so a bucket brigade had been started. That's where I spotted my father.

Dad was manning the pump when suddenly he felt something tugging at him. He looked down to find his youngest daughter clinging to his pant legs and crying her eyes out. A friend was sent to find Mother and take her place in the bucket line so she could take me to a nearby house where Love and Lowene were watching the activity.

When the fire trucks arrived, Manilla's pumper had to get water from Mud Creek behind the store, but Rushville's truck had a tank of chemicals to fight the blaze. The main brick building had only smoke damage but the ice cream parlor was gutted. The charred remains were torn down and never rebuilt.

The Secret in Our Basement

Our house had no electricity until around the time I started sixth grade. Before then we studied by kerosene lamps. Then Dad bought a gas-powered generator for our basement to power electricity. Knowing little bout such machinery, he hired a neighbor named Bill to maintain the generator.

Unfortunately Dad also kept in the basement a five gallon jug of whiskey he used for medical purposes. He assumed his hiding place was safe until the day mother came face to face with

Bill as he was leaving the cellar and the odor of liquor nearly knocked her off her feet. After that, Dad had to find a new hiding place for his *special medicine*.

Foxy Grandpa Surfaces Again

Eventually electricity became available and Dad decided we needed it in our barn, our house and his office. At the time, you had to pay the electric company to install equipment and string power lines to a new area. He tried to get other Homer residents to share the cost of all that, thus making the project cheaper for everyone, but no one would go in with him.

He learned why when he overheard several people discussing the situation. It seemed the others had decided to let Doctor Barnett foot the entire bill for bringing the electricity into town, then pay the cheaper fee to attach to an existing line.

When Dad told the electrical company what he'd learned, the company decided to put in a transformer only large enough for our needs. As a result, by the time the others applied for service, they found they not only had to pay for another line, but also a big transformer. In the end, they paid almost double the original cost without assistance from Foxy Doctor Barnett.

We still used our old generator for backup whenever the lines were down during a storm. Natural gas wells were common in our area, so we used gas for the new range that replaced our original wood burning stove. For a long time I missed the warmth from that old stove. In bad weather the gas lines often froze up and we couldn't always draw a good flame.

The Doctor's Wife

You've probably noted that my father was the dominant parent in our family. But don't get the impression that Mother did not have a personality or a strong character, for she was a force to be reckoned with.

While she did not discipline with an iron hand, she was very firm about anything she felt might harm us. And when she said no it meant *NO*. Her approach to child rearing was to be firm when faced with a major problem, but tread lightly on minor matters. Often she simply pointed out to whichever offspring was misbehaving that altering their behavior was the quickest way to avoid serious punishment.

As I think back on my sweet mother I'm amazed. Even years later, at eighty, she could out-work and out-last me, astounding when you consider what her life required her to be:

Wife. Mother to four children. Secretary and bookkeeper for a busy medical practice. Part-time nurse. Loving daughter-in-law. Gardener. Homemaker. Office cleaning lady. And laundress for both her family's needs and Dad's office linens.

Every summer Mom also canned vegetables for the winter and ran what amounted to a nursing home for the many relatives who swooped down on her at various times.

Aunts, uncles and cousins came to visit and enlist Dad to treat (for free, of course) current ailments. Our house was small, so we children had to yield our beds to the adults and older cousins. All four of us slept on pallets on the floor of the porch that wrapped around two sides of the house. On rainy nights we crowded into the house with everyone else.

My mother was also a fabulous cook. Her pies and cakes and other desserts were scrumptious (which probably added to the popularity of her summer boarding house.) Her fried chicken and roasts were very good too. Of course she had good foods to start with since we raised most of what we needed. Dad often brought home oranges and bananas to add variety to our diet.

The Crooked-mouth Family

Homer's church groups and lodges liked to include entertainment in their programs. During her elocution lessons, Mom had learned a special little recitation - complete with appropriate facial movements - that groups often asked her to present. Her presentation was called the "Crooked-Mouth Family" and sometimes she'd do it for us. This is the way it went:

Pa could only talk out of the right side of his mouth. (Mother delivered this line with her own mouth twisted to the right side.) Ma could only talk out of the left side of her mouth. (Delivered with her mouth twisted to the left.) Brother could only talk through the bottom of his mouth. (Here, she spoke with her lower lip extended.) Big Sister could only talk through the top of her mouth. (Said with upper lip extended over her pulled-in lower lip.) Only Baby Sister had a perfect little mouth and could speak very clearly. (Spoken in a normal manner.)

When it was time for bed, each of the first four members of the family tried to blow out the candle. (Using each facial contortion in turn, Mother held up an index finger as the imaginary candle and attempted to it blow out. Of course, each family member's puff of air came out in the wrong direction, making the task impossible.) But Baby Sister with her straight little mouth saved the day. She blew out the candle in just - one - puff. End of presentation.

Candles in the Darkness

Once again Mom had been pressed into service to direct a church program; this time for the summer Bible school. In the final presentation of the evening, a group of pre-teen girls (myself included) were to walk from the back of the sanctuary to the front, wearing gauzy white costumes and carrying lighted candles. Once there, we were to form a tableau.

Mother had purchased special candles for this, each producing a different colored smoke. If all went as planned, when she lit the candles, the rainbow of smoke against our white costumes and the flickering candles we carried would be the highlight of the evening.

We girls had spent the entire Bible school interval as helpers for the toddlers and pre-schoolers. The last thing any of us wanted to do was be in a *b-o-r-i-n-g* pageant.

This event took place on a humid June night with windows open to capture as much breeze as possible. The planning committee had made our costumes and provided our candles; however, they hadn't anticipated the side effects of a hot night and open windows.

The lights went out and we and our flickering candles became the target of June bugs. They got in our hair, caught in our gauzy robes and pinched us. Talk about contortionists!

As we marched to the music, we squirmed and hit and stabbed and swatted. By the moment it came time to stand still for the tableau, the audience was howling with laughter. It was a miracle none of us went up in flames. Boring, it wasn't.

Battling the Elements

Indiana winters could be severe. After one blizzard snow drifted against our doors, shutting us in. Dad, who was a little over six feet, had to climb out a window into a drift that came up to his arm pits so he could clear a path to his office, several yards from the house. He maintained his own pharmacy and had to keep the base burner going to keep the medicines from freezing.

After Dad cleared the snow from the doors, my brother had to battle the drifts to get to the barn so he could feed and water the horse and take care of the cow we kept for fresh milk.

In addition to aspiring to racehorse status, Pet had learned to lift her stall's latch. During yet another storm Dad came in quite late from tending a patient to find the horse gone. Dad was exhausted, so he woke Doc, told him to get dressed and find Pet.

Doc pulled on his boots, went out the front door without a coat, then walked through the snow around the porch and came in the side door. He said, "Brrr, it's cold," pulled off his boots, and went right back to bed without ever waking up.

At that point, Dad decided if the horse was dumb enough to leave a warm stall to go out in a snow storm she could just stay out. The next morning we found Pet back in her stall. After that, Dad put a better latch on her door.

SIX

HOW WE CHILDREN SPENT OUR TIME

The summer I was nine, Dad bought a Model T Ford and I began to go with him on his rounds. Whenever we reached a heavy gate leading to a patient's home, Dad would get out and open the gate, then let me drive through. At smaller gates, he drove and I did the opening and closing.

Sometimes Dad would find he didn't have the necessary medicine in his bag. When this happened, he'd return home and prepare the medicine from his own pharmacy. Then he'd send me back to the farmer to deliver the pills or liquid or salve.

Once he sent me on such an errand before I had mastered the art of backing up. He told me that there was a long lane up to the house, but there was also a big barn lot where I could turn around to come home. I took the Arbuckle's visiting granddaughter, seven-year-old Diddy Carr, along for company.

Everything was fine until we reached the lot, which was now filled with threshing machines and wagons, leaving no room to turn around. The farmer, not realizing my predicament, took the medicine and hurried back inside to rejoin his farm hands and finish eating dinner. He left behind one surprised child who had no choice but to attempt to back down the lane.

There was a ditch on one side of the lane and a cornfield on the other. Diddy looked out the back window and would say, "Go left. Now go right." Since my right was her left, and vice versa, after a while she became a little confused. Eventually, we came so close to disaster that I yelled, "Hold on, Diddy, we're going in the ditch!"

At that point I decided it would be safer to turn around in the cornfield. I drove into the field and cut a big swath through the knee-high corn, then veered back onto the lane and continued on home. It was hard to juggle the clutch and the throttle and keep that old Ford running. If the engine had died, I would have been in a fine pickle, for it had to be cranked to restart it and I was not strong enough to do it.

Dad's next car, purchased when I was about eleven, had a self-starter. Without telling Dad, I practiced driving up and back in the lane next to the house until I could shift without stripping the gears. Rather than getting mad when he discovered what I was doing, Dad began letting me drive on the road, especially when he had confinement (childbirth) cases late at night. I drove and he slept. The gravel roads were often badly rutted and very hard to negotiate but somehow I managed.

My Day at the Spa

French Lick and West Baden in southern Indiana were noted for their mineral water spas. This water tasted awful and smelled even worse, but was thought to cure a variety of ailments. Another place called Mudlavia advertised hot springs that they claimed would cure rheumatism.

Several of Dad's patients wanted him to take them to Mudlavia to try the hot mud baths. He decided that mother and I should go along and stay in the resort's lodge.

The man who owned or managed the place was called the Colonel and lived in a big house. I can still vividly remember two rooms in his home -- the den and the sun room. Apparently he'd been on safaris because both were filled with tiger, lion and other wild game heads. I found it very depressing.

I was about nine at the time, so the Colonel asked Dad if I could come up to the house to play with his granddaughter who was a year or two older. The girl was being tutored because she'd missed some school. When I arrived, she was reciting her multiplication tables and was on the fours and fives.

The Colonel asked if I knew my tables. Because Dad was a mathematician and emphasized the basics, I was well drilled in that area. Not realizing how the other girl would react, I immediately recited the fours and continued on through the nines without being prompted. The Colonel complemented me on being such a good student, but his granddaughter was furious at what she saw as being shown up.

When the girl was free, we went to play in a carriage house filled with very ornate and highly decorated surreys and sleighs and buggies. It was fun climbing in all the vehicles, pretending to drive them. During a game of hide and seek, my new playmate disappeared and I discovered I'd been locked in.

At first I didn't worry. But soon it began to get dark, so I crawled into a big carriage where I felt safe and went to sleep. I'd been told that they used one of the vehicles to get the mail early in the morning, so I knew I'd be found eventually.

As time passed and I didn't appear for dinner, Dad began a search. First he called the Colonel whose granddaughter denied any knowledge of my whereabouts. Later, when they found me asleep in the locked building, she finally admitted she'd locked me in. After that, my parents wouldn't let me play with her.

Dr. Barnett Increases His Holdings

In addition to the house in Homer, Dad purchased two farms as both an investment and to insure we always had good meat and fresh produce. On one farm we raised hogs and fruit and had a huge garden. The second farm included a beautiful old three-story house where we raised first dairy, then beef cattle.

Since we raised our own livestock, we butchered at least twice a year. Our smokehouse was actually an enclosed cupboard attached to the kitchen in Homer where we hickory smoked our pork and hams and cured bacon. We shared everything we raised with the two couples who lived on and tended the farms.

At home we had a Jersey cow that my brother milked. It gave such rich milk that the cream on top of a gallon of milk would be over an inch thick. When Grandmother Miller visited us she liked to churn. She would then sell the butter to neighbors and earn a little spending money for all her labor.

My sister Love liked the cream to whip for deserts, but she had to get to it before Grandmother did. Once she was getting some cream and Dad stole in behind her. Love jumped and said, "Oh, it's you! I thought it was Grandmother."

When Mother realized that Dad also enjoyed his shortcakes with whipped cream, she explained to Grandmother that she would have to share her precious cream. Grandmother said, "I just didn't want any of it to go to waste."

Dad could have assured her nothing would be wasted. We children had been taught to take small servings, both at home and when visiting, and to eat everything we put on our plates.

Shortly after coming to Homer Dad had joined the Masonic and Redman Lodges. Often the groups would have pitch-in dinners or oyster stew suppers. Dad always bragged that he could pick out our empty plates from among all the others.

Later we bought pasteurized milk and cream from a dairy, but it was never as good as that cream from our own Jersey cow.

Enjoying the Fruits of Our Labor

In our garden at home we grew grapes, both white and purple and every kind of vegetable you might name. We had a rhubarb bed that Mother turned into sauce and pies.

Dad believed that celery was more tender when it was white. To keep the sun from triggering the chlorophyll that turns it green, we wrapped newspaper around the stalks. Later Dad bought round tiles which had been rejected as imperfect. These were much easier than tying papers around dozens of plants. I think Dad's theory must have been right, because those white celery stalks, as well as the white asparagus shoots we dug up before they turned green were especially tender.

My garden job was debugging new potato plants. I knocked the bugs off each plant into a solution called Paris Green. I worked hard, but hated that job. To this day, I'm not fond of new red potatoes, even when cooked with onions and bacon and fresh green beans the way Mother used to fix them.

We also raised chickens and had our own eggs. Periodically, Mother would sell off most of the old hens and keep some of the young pullets. We enjoyed fried or baked or stewed chicken with dumplings quite often.

Between our garden and small orchard in Homer and larger plots at the two farms, we harvested enough produce to can our year's supply of vegetables. The farm manager prepared the ground, then we furnished and planted the seed and tilled the soil. The harvest was then shared by both families.

The farm also had blackberry, dewberry, and raspberry patches that provided fruit for wonderful jellies and jams. The huge strawberry bed once yielded two bushel baskets in one picking. With so much fruit, we decided to throw a party.

Dad belonged to the county and state medical societies, so he invited the members and wives of both groups to a strawberry feast. Mother and I baked angel food cakes and ordered ice cream. So many reservations came in, we had to ask neighbors to help us prepare. Members of Mother's home economics organization helped by baking cakes, preparing berries and serving. In order to seat everyone, we rented chairs and tables and set them up in the house, on the porch and all over the lawn. We served seventy-five people that day and most of the men had seconds.

A Special Friendship

When I was about nine, one of Dad's friends died. His widow was earning her living by making quilts, but was afraid to be alone at night, so Dad sent Love to stay with the woman. After a while, Love said she didn't like staying there, so I took her place every evening after supper.

Aunt Laura (as I was taught to call her) had no children but loved me like I was her own and spoiled me rotten while I was there. Some of the neighbor children began coming by to play with me in the big orchard beside her home. Eventually all the kids in Homer joined us.

I made up many of the games we played. One, which I called Hot Butter and Blue Beans, was a combination of tag and hide and seek that involved the use of fronds from Iris plants. Where that name came from I can never remember.

Aunt Laura would sit on her porch and watch us play charades and tag and run and laugh and have a wonderful time. Dad became worried and asked her if she wanted him to stop all the noise. She said, "No, because that *noise* is the sweetest sound I've ever heard. There is no quarreling, just laughter."

Aunt Laura had beautiful marble-topped furniture throughout her house. When I admired one special dresser, she told me that someday I would have that piece and one of her quilts as a thank you for staying with her. Later, while I was away at college, she became ill and her nieces, who'd never visited until her illness, came and took all her belongings away.

Shortly after that, I went to see her. She cried and said, "I should have given you the quilt and dresser before I got sick."

Gently, I explained that I had no place to put such things, then assured her I would always remember how lovely they were in her home and would never forget how much love she'd given me. I never saw her again.

The Substitute Nurse

I was about ten or eleven when Dad asked me to assist in an operation. A small boy had lost a finger when he grabbed the rope of a pulley that was lifting hay to the loft. His mother, who was a nurse, was going to administer the anesthesia, but because she was also pregnant, she fainted.

Dad called me over from the house to fill in. We sterilized our hands and he taught me how to drop anesthesia (probably ether or chloroform) onto the cone over the boy's nose. After the operation we cleaned everything up together.

Later when I was about thirteen or fourteen and my sisters were away at college, my maternal grandmother died. While Mom was in Iowa for the funeral, I kept house for Dad. One night around midnight the injured teenagers from a car accident were brought to Dad to stitch up. Again, I had to administer the anesthesia.

Dad started me getting one patient under while he sterilized his instruments and cleaned the boy's other wounds. When he was finally out, Dad took twelve stitches. Another teen required two stitches and two others needed wounds cleaned and bandaged before we could call their parents to come for them.

From Nurse to Scrub Woman

My regular job was cleaning the office. The wooden operating table had to be washed and polished. Its leather cushion then had to be draped with sheets and covered with a bolt of white paper that was rolled out and torn off between each patient. The sheets had to be changed daily (or more often if fluids seeped through the paper) then washed and boiled and hung in the sun to dry or in our basement in winter.

I also scrubbed the floor, polished the furniture, and cleaned the pharmacy. Even in larger towns that had a drug store, most doctors maintained a pharmacy in their own office. Sometimes the store would be closed or too far away for a sick patient or his family to travel. Also, many medicines of the time had to be mixed to order.

The gallon jugs in the pharmacy were easy to clean, but the small bottles were tedious. I had to use a strong disinfectant to wash them and then wipe each one. In comparison, the waiting room was simple to care for, just dusting and mopping once or twice a week. When I was in school, I did all this after I got home or on the weekends. Sometimes Mother had to help.

Doc Goes to High School

Because he started school before he was five, Doc was a just shy of thirteen when Dad sent him to Shelbyville High School as a freshman. Even so, he was already six feet tall. When he and sixteen year old neighbor Loren Hodges who was six two went out for freshman basketball, Coach Tim Campbell looked at both boys and said, "They certainly grow them tall in Homer."

The train to Shelbyville that the boys rode would whistle a mile down the track to give them time to cross the pasture behind our house and get on the other side of the tracks.

Mr. Miranda, the conductor, had a son at the University of Michigan and knew Dad who often sent medicine to Manilla or Rays Crossing or Shelbyville which Mr. Miranda then delivered to waiting patients.

As a junior, Doc was cast as Willie in the play "Seventeen" to be performed at Shelbyville's City Hall auditorium. My contribution to the production was playing all the other parts so Doc could rehearse. The performance was so well received an extra night was added to the scheduled run.

In one scene Willie was supposed to read a poem, but the person in charge of props had forgotten to put the paper in Doc's jacket pocket. Improvising, he announced, "I must have left it in the car." A moment later he returned to the stage, read the poem, and the play continued. Only those who had seen one of the previous performances knew about the goof.

Frances Repeats the Wrong Thing

Somehow Doc had escaped the mumps when he was younger, so when I had them, he caught them from me. At the time, he was playing on the baseball team for Coach Campbell. Although my own case was mild, Doc was very ill.

I heard Dad remark to Mother that he was worried the mumps might "go down" on Doc. (A term for a complication in which the virus that triggers the disease causes inflammation in a boy's testicles or girl's ovaries and in rare cases causes sterility.)

Because I was only in seventh grade, I didn't understand the meaning of the phrase, so when Coach Campbell asked about Doc, I repeated Dad's remark. The coach got very red in the face, so I asked Dad to define his comment as soon as I got home. After he explained, I had a hard time facing Coach Campbell for some time. In retrospect I'm sure he was aware of how innocent I was and was just as embarrassed for me.

Missionaries in the Family

Mother's cousin Paul Wiant and his wife were missionaries to China where Paul was an engineer and built roads and bridges for the Chinese government. Because Paul's wife was ill, the couple had returned home with their two children to ask Dad to evaluate her health.

The first night after the children were put to bed, as I passed the bedroom door I recognized the song they were singing in a Chinese dialect. It seems they sang themselves to sleep each night. Their little voices were lovely, but hearing "Jesus Loves Me" in another language was certainly startling. As missionaries Paul and his wife had to teach the Chinese peasants habits we Americans considered basic. With little concept of the connection between sanitation and disease, many watered their gardens by urinating on the plants. Paul had to build a very high fence to prevent passers-by from irrigating his own garden.

Left: Frances Barnett, about age 1, in front of the family garden.
Below: Frances Barnett and unknown neighbor, possibly Bobby Frow

Frances Barnett in Homer,
c. 1920s

Dr. Daniel E. Barnett in Homer,
late 1920s or early 1930s

At right: Irma Lowene Barnett, high school graduation photo

Below: Inez Love Barnett Upjohn, at her summer home in Gull Lake, MI, c. late 1930s

Arthur R. Barnett, probably his college graduation photo

Frances Marie Barnett, 1929 Shelbyville High School Squib yearbook photo

SEVEN

MY SIBLINGS' LIVES

Love was pretty and vivacious and had lots of dates when she went to the University of Michigan. One outing illustrates the poise and grace she always displayed in unexpected situations.

Ann Arbor was very cold and girls often wore long johns covered by bloomers. As Love and her date walked along, the elastic waist of her bloomers broke and fell down around her ankles. Without skipping a beat, she calmly stepped out of the bloomers, handed them to her date to put in his overcoat pocket, and went on. At the end of the evening she thanked her escort for a lovely evening and retrieved her bloomers.

Love Gets Stood Up

One summer when Love was home from college, a young man she'd met at a party asked her to a movie. The night of their date Mother and Dad were entertaining friends whose tiny baby's crying was preventing the young mother from eating her dinner. While she waited for her date, Love carried the infant into the living room, fed it a bottle, then rocked the baby to sleep.

The young man who was picking her up got to the house earlier than he'd planned. After parking his car, he peeked into the living room window and saw Love with the now sleeping baby. Thinking she was playing with a doll and was much younger than he'd thought, he drove away without coming in.

Love was furious at being stood up. When the boy learned of his mistake, he called to apologize and asked for another chance. I don't think he knew what hit him. Love told him in no uncertain terms that he'd had no business peeking in windows. And that furthermore, a true gentleman would have knocked on the door and ascertained the situation.

My oldest sister did not suffer fools.

Love Changes Dad's Mind

While she was at college, Love learned to play bridge. She had inherited Dad's mathematical mind and enjoyed figuring out the placement of the high cards in the game. During her next vacation, rather than go out one evening she invited her date and another couple to the house to play bridge.

Dad's religious upbringing had forbidden gambling and he associated cards with poker and other games of chance. When he realized what was going on, he ordered the game stopped.

Love calmly explained that there was no betting involved and described the mathematical challenges bridge presented. Once he'd played few games himself, Dad allowed her to continue playing with her friends.

Soon after Love returned to college, Mother and Dad began playing bridge with Bill and Gladys English. One month Mom would fix dinner for the foursome; the next month the other couple would entertain. There was little to do in Homer, so the new routine was a pleasant diversion.

The Legacy of a Random Act of Kindness

We were about to sit down to dinner one Sunday when a man knocked on our door and asked for my father. Dad recognized him immediately as the student he had found a college job and housing and bought clothing for during his teaching days. The man pressed some money into Dad's hand and said, "I owe you far more than that."

Dad refused to take the money, telling his former pupil, "Just help some other student as I helped you."

Since the visitor's wife and daughter were with him, Dad invited the family to eat with us. During dinner, Dad learned that his former student was now teaching chemistry at the high school in New Castle, Indiana, about thirty miles from Homer.

At the time, Love had just gotten her teaching certificate and was looking for a position. Thus, much to the man's delight, he was able to recommend that the daughter of his former mentor be hired to teach botany and math in his own school.

Sister of the Bride

One of Love's classmates at Michigan, a med student named Gifford Upjohn, hadn't known her name, but wanted to meet her. Eventually, he found someone to introduce them. Things progressed nicely from there and shortly before I graduated from high school, he and Love were married in a beautiful ceremony in Rushville.

Gifford's sister Esther, one of Love's fellow teachers at New Castle, and one of her college sorority sisters served as bridesmaids and Lowene was Maid of Honor. Dad's lawyer, Chauncy Duncan, and his wife gave a luncheon for the family and the wedding reception was held in the church parlor.

Gifford's family came from New Jersey to attend the wedding and proved to be charming people. His mother Gratia learned that one of her college friends lived in Shelbyville and they had an opportunity to see each other. Besides Esther, Gifford had another sister and a younger brother Allen who was about eleven. For some unknown reason, Allen took a liking to me and stuck to my side like glue throughout the visit.

Our home was small and, since there were no hotels in Homer and no really decent ones in nearby towns, everyone stayed with us and various neighbors who offered their guest rooms. I'm afraid many guests found things very countrified.

Nevertheless, we all lived through the marriage ceremony, I managed to survive Allen's attentions and Love and Gif went off to the Rockies on their honeymoon. Then they returned to Ann Arbor where Gifford interned at the hospital and Love began work on her masters.

A Mischievous Nephew

Harold, Love's first child, was born while she was still in college. She and Gifford moved to Kalamazoo when Harold was about two years old. As Love was packing for their overnight stay at a hotel, Harold apparently decided she was going without him. Love turned around to discover that he had thrown every thing out of the suitcase and was stretched out in the bag ready to go.

Soon after their move, Love and Gif completed their family with the birth of their daughter Nancy.

My Sister Lowene

Although she was a very good student, Lowene wasn't as aggressive as Love, perhaps because Mother so clearly favored her older sister. Miss. Kinsley, who taught all three of us in high school, once said to me that Love learned very easily, but just as easily forgot much of whatever she found uninteresting, while Lowene retained everything she learned for life.

Lowene crocheted and knitted and did tatting. She also sewed clothes for my dolls. Dad's foxy streak came out in her as well. When I was a small baby, she often intentionally woke me just before it was time to wash dishes so Mother would ask her to take care of me instead.   Then, as I got older, we often sat side by side on the front porch while she read her favorite books such as Les Misérables aloud to me.

Very petite (not quite five feet tall), Lowene had a beautiful smile and a cute little giggle and gorgeous grey eyes.

While Love had Mabel Hiner for a friend, Lowene had Helen Mull. Lowene had learned to drive Dad's model A Ford. One day as she was returning from taking Helen home, she had to turn aside for an obstruction in the road and lost control and went into a deep ditch. Luckily she was unhurt and able to walk home. Dad retrieved the car, but unfortunately didn't make Lowene get right back in and drive. I was a grown woman before she summoned the nerve to begin driving again.

A Tough Time to Be a Student

Both my sisters attended Michigan at the same time although, because of the way their birth dates fell, Love was a couple of years ahead of Lowene.

By the time Lowene entered, Dad was feeling the effects of the impending depression. Farm prices were dropping and Dad was losing money. In addition to his own farming woes, many of his patients were farmers. Those that weren't, depended as Dad did on the services or purchases paid for by farmers.

To help Dad with expenses, Lowene took a reduced course load and worked in the catalog department of the university's library. Although she finally received her B.A. after several years, Dad's finances eventually became so bad that she had to abandon her studies before completing her library degree.

Lowene was an excellent cataloger, so the department head at the university recommended her for similar position with the Detroit Public Library. Although she was no longer in school, she set aside a portion of her wages to help Doc, and later me, continue our education.

Lowene Baby Sits

When our niece Nancy was about sixteen months old, Love and Gifford asked Lowene to baby sit their two children. As they started to drive off, Love noticed Nancy pick up a pebble and stick it in her mouth. The Upjohns' last look of their children and their sitter was of Lowene holding Nancy by her heels until the pebble fell out of her mouth. Gif looked at Love and said, "It's obvious the kids are in good hands."

Despite her great love of children, Lowene was destined to remain childless. Some years after she began working in Detroit, the removal of a large fibroid tumor from her womb ended her hopes for a family. It was a hard blow for the young woman who, as a young girl, wanted a black baby to care for, but settled for a towheaded sister to whom she read classic literature.

Carelessness Causes a Serious Injury

With his two older sisters out of the house and the pesky tag-along no longer dogging his steps, Doc was enjoying his high school years. Part of his happiest times were spent playing sports. That is, until he became the victim of a lab mishap.

During a lecture, Doc's high school chemistry teacher was demonstrating the properties of phosphorus magnesium. Proper procedure called for the substance to be placed under water before it was processed. But the teacher was distracted and failed to take that precaution. Suddenly, sparks flew and a girl's skirt caught on fire.

Someone noticed that Doc's pants were also aflame. Another student grabbed a pitcher of water and put the fire out, but not before Doc sustained a very deep burn on his calf. By the time the teacher had regained enough of his composure to cover the chemical with water and yell for everyone to evacuate the room, the students were already out.

The wound healed slowly. Four weeks later, Doc was on the mend, but he'd missed the rest of the baseball season.

Basketball: Hoosier Hysteria

Doc also played basketball all the way through high school. One year the team went to the final level of Indiana's state tournament. There, an even smaller school named Milan beat them by holding the ball instead of running plays. (In the twenties, there was no rule to prevent such tactics.)

Although Milan ultimately failed to win the championship that year, in the fifties, they beat a school even larger than Shelbyville to capture the title. Their play that season was so impressive it later inspired the movie "Hoosiers."

One year when my grandmother was on her annual visit, she attended one of Doc's games with us. When it was over and we were waiting to take him home, Grandmother walked out on the court and looked up at the hoop. Just then the coach came out and asked what she was thinking. She said that she didn't see how they got that big ball to go through that little hoop. Coach Campbell smiled and said, "Practice, Practice!"

Doc's Summer Jobs

During one summer break from high school, Doc worked in the hayfields for the father of one of Love's friends. One evening Doc told Dad that his employer had asked him to put up two things that looked like crosses. Dad shushed him up and said, "It isn't any of our business." The next day Doc learned that the Ku Klux Klan had held a rally on the farm and burned the crosses. Thankfully, those evil robes had disappeared from our hall closet many years earlier.

My brother spent his summer break after his freshman year at the University of Michigan with Lowene in Detroit. There he earned money for his next semester by delivering ice. His job often required that he climb to third floor apartments carrying blocks of ice weighing one hundred and fifty to two hundred pounds. His clothing was constantly soaked.

Going between summer heat and the chill of the ice house in wet clothes eventually took its toll. By the time Doc began his sophomore year, the cold he'd tried to ignore had worsened. Now gravely ill, he was admitted to the university hospital.

The staff called Dad and told him that Doc was dying. A second call from Love's husband Gifford confirmed that the situation was indeed that serious. The year was 1926. The Great Depression was looming ever closer and now my brother was lying near death miles from home.

Normally Dad would never have considered getting into what amounted to an experimental two-seater bi-plane that a patient named Tat Lower had constructed. But Tat *had* taken flying lessons, so Dad asked Tat to fly him to Ann Arbor.

When he reached the hospital, Dad insisted that the labs run additional tests and quickly determined that, in addition to pneumonia, Doc had a kidney disease called nephritis. They started IV's and forced Doc to drink gallons of water.

Doc was scared, but Dad told him, "Son, you're not going to die, but you have a tough row ahead of you." Before the IVs and the forced fluids, Doc's fever had been 105 degrees. By that evening his temperature had fallen dramatically.

Dad was exhausted, so he went to Doc's fraternity to rest. Knowing Dad's fear of large dogs, Doc had warned him about the fraternity's mascot, a great Dane named Thor, who was also used as a watch dog. With great trepidation, Dad opened the door. Thor raised his head, then immediately went back to sleep. A grateful Dad stretched out on one of the frat house's sofas and fell asleep instantly.

As soon as he was well enough to travel, Dad brought my brother home to Indiana to recuperate.

A Long Recovery

A large part of the cure for nephritis was complete bed rest and Doc quickly became bored. He continued to drink gallons of water and fruit juices. I was a freshman that year, so to keep him occupied, I began checking books out of the Shelbyville library for him before I came home.

Doc had never really had time to read for pleasure before. Soon he discovered O'Henry's short stories and became an avid reader. I brought him biographies and adventure and mysteries and historical novels, anything anyone suggested. He spent his days reading, but by evening he wanted to play games. I played "Knock Knock" games until I began to hate them.

Another down side to his prescribed regimen was a tasteless diet. He was allowed neither salt nor protein, since both must be processed by the kidneys.

At Thanksgiving he begged for turkey. Dad cut a very small piece of the breast and mother hid it under the mashed potatoes and gravy. Doc looked the plate over and seeing no turkey, said, "Take it away."

I said, "You give up too easily." Did he ever dig into those unsalted potatoes and bland gravy to find that hidden treasure.

After his health improved, Doc returned to Michigan to continue his sophomore year.

Doggy Breath

During school breaks, members of Doc's fraternity rotated responsibility for housing their mascot. Doc's turn to care for the great Dane came over Christmas. One of the boys wasn't using his small coupe during the holidays so Doc drove it home. Thor rode in the tiny car's back seat with his head hanging over Doc's shoulder. Since the dog had an extreme case of halitosis, as well as a tendency to drool, the trip was anything but pleasant.

When the car quit running in a little-known town called Philadelphia, Indiana, Doc called Dad to come and get him. There was some momentary confusion as Dad demanded to know what Doc was doing in Pennsylvania.

It was a good thing we had butchered about that time because Thor nearly ate us out of house and home. The dog was adept at opening doors and let himself out of the house whenever he needed to do his daily business. He slept in Doc's room which he guarded fiercely the entire time he was there. Thor kept an eye on Doc as well. One night Doc planned to go out, but had a devil of a time getting away from his bodyguard to go pick up his date.

Mother had her own encounter with Thor.

Our house had one big central heating unit in the floor. When Doc's door was shut, his room got very chilly. Mom knew that Doc would be cold when he came home, so she started to open the door of his room. As she did, Thor rose and growled. Mom quickly shut the door and told him, "Just freeze then."

I couldn't help thinking about that Christmas many years later when a friend and I stopped at a Dairy Queen in Indianapolis on a very hot night. As we ate our ice cream, a red convertible drove up next to us. In the passenger seat was a great Dane. As the young driver returned with his ice cream, the dog lunged and gobbled the triple dip cone in one bite.

One look at the expression on the driver's face and we were in hysterics. The boy returned for another triple dip, but this time he stood near the building and ate it. When he came back to the car he said, "Bad dog."

When that great Dane hung his head as if he was really sorry, I didn't believe it for a moment.

A Dream Dies

My brother's dream was to follow Dad into medicine. But after Doc's kidney illness, Dad knew that it would be many years before Doc's health would completely return to normal. The chance that the rigors of med school might trigger a relapse were too great, so, reluctantly, Doc switched his major to teaching with an emphasis on health and biology.

One summer Doc took summer courses at an Illinois school that toured in a bus known as a university on wheels. The first year he went east to learn about the geography and history of that area. He found it was a wonderful learning experience, so the next year he did it again, this time going west.

The class traveled the southern route and then up the coast to Canada. Most of the students were teachers getting refresher courses, as was Doc, who manned the movie camera for their professor whose teenage son had come along.

When they arrived at Canada's Lake Louise, Doc and two other teachers and the professor's son took a marked and fairly easy trail up the mountain. Once at the top, the boy insisted on starting down a much more hazardous path, ignoring the warning of the adults. Within moments, he lost his footing, slipped over the side and landed on a ledge.

Although not physically injured, the rebellious teen refused to cooperate when they tried help him back up. One teacher went back down the marked trail to get help. Doc and the other man stayed behind to calm the boy, who was now quite agitated and in danger of slipping even farther down the side of the mountain.

The sun kept sinking lower and the thought of being trapped by darkness wasn't very appealing. Because they'd been studying land formations, the two men were able to determine that the ledge the boy was on was one of a series that led to the bottom of the mountain. They decided to join the teen and attempt to lead him to safety.

Once as they rested on an especially narrow ledge, a section of rock broke off. Doc listened as it skidded off the lower ledges and finally hit bottom. He told us he immediately thought of his home and family and all the things he hoped to do and realized that death could be only a misstep away.

As darkness began to fall, the ledges gave way to a solid terrain with a gradual slope that made walking much easier. But now they had to watch for bear caves and holes that might trip them. It was dark by the time they got back to camp and the teenager immediately made himself scarce.

The professor, who had left camp to visit friends, had just been located and had returned to gather a search party. He began berating Doc for letting his son start down the unmarked trail. As Doc defended himself, the other two teachers set the professor straight about his son's behavior.

One of the guides who'd been called out to lead the search party then talked to the boy and also revealed that only weeks before, a Purdue University professor and his wife had perished on that same trail. Doc said at that news, his high altitude musings took on new meaning.

EIGHT

GOING TO SCHOOL IN SHELBYVILLE

While our school in Homer included twelve grades, it did not offer the courses Dad knew we would need to prepare for a college education. Thus, Love and Lowene transferred to Shelbyville High School and graduated from there. Because it was too far to drive a buggy, they rode the train to school.

Dad chose Shelbyville rather than Rushville simply because the train traveled that directions each morning. In the afternoons, it made its return trip shortly after school let out.

As freshmen, Doc and his best friend Loren Hodges also transferred to SHS. When Dad decided to pay the extra two years' tuition to send me to seventh grade at Shelbyville Junior High, I joined the boys on the train. By now Doc realized there was just no way to completely rid his life of his tag-along little sister.

Adjusting from a one-room class to a campus-like situation was not easy. Love suggested that I pick out one girl in my class and follow her lead. I chose Frances Fisher and became her shadow until I learned my way around.

My home room teacher was a Mr. Gifford. Since my name began with a B, I was seated toward the front of the room. For some reason, those particular seats were set lower than the ones nearer the back. At five foot four, I was not especially tall, but I had to sit on my spine to even get into the seat.

About the second day of school, Mr. Gifford came to my desk and asked, "Did they not teach you to sit up straight in Homer?" I replied, "Yes, they did. But they gave me a seat tall enough that I could get my legs under the desk."

He examined my chair and immediately called maintenance to raise not only my desk, but several more for other students who now felt brave enough to also complain. Two of the taller boys had been forced to straddle their seats.

Mr. Gifford seemed surprised at my aggressiveness. I think he expected the little towhead from the country school to be a meek little thing.

Working My Way Through

Because of the possibility that the train might be late, I was assigned no first hour class. Instead, I worked in the principal's office. My duties were to pick up attendance slips, answer the phone and take messages, especially those from mothers calling with excuses for their children's ill health or tardiness.

Through the noon hour and during fifth period, I also worked in the cafeteria, slinging hash so to speak. I soon knew the teachers in both junior and senior High. They all begged me to save them some kind of tidbits, like chicken livers or special pieces of chicken. Rather than risk playing favorites, I quickly learned to smile and say, "Couldn't do it today."

I got a free lunch for taking this second job. Doc was a Junior and a big basketball star. All the eighth grade girls had crushes on him and pestered me, wanting introductions to my big brother. When I told Doc, he thought it was all a big joke.

Rather than wait at the train station after school, I would often go to the cafeteria to study. Miss. Mull, who ran the cafeteria and taught home economics, also lived in Homer. Many times she would hand me a list and ask me to order items for the next day's noon meal. This meant calling the butcher, the ice cream parlor and the grocery stores.

Since my office work and hash slinging duties took up so much of my time, I had little time to study and took most of my books home with me. Doc said I looked like a walking library.

After Frances Fisher and I became friends, I was allowed to go to her home after school so we could go to the basketball games together. Dad would then come in from Homer to drive Doc and me home after the game.

The Perils of Riding the Train

I sometimes found that as a commuting student, I faced problems others didn't. Once, I was supposed to read a chapter from a non-circulating book for a class, but by the time I finished my other duties a boy from my class was monopolizing the text. It quickly became obvious that he was purposely dawdling and had no intention of letting me complete the assignment.

Knowing I had to get to the train soon, I explained the situation to the librarian and she made him give me the book. I scanned the chapter hurriedly, then checked the time, realized I was in trouble and I began running as fast I could.

Partway there, Doc met me and practically carried me the rest of the way. The conductor, Mr. Miranda, was provoked. In a gruff voice he told me that he had oiled every cog, every wheel and some other places that didn't need oiling, as well as backed up twice for water and would have left me in another moment.

"If an inspector had been on this train, I would have lost my job. What kept you?"

Once I explained my predicament and he realized I hadn't been fooling around, he was much more cordial.

Frances Asserts Herself

While my sister Love taught at New Castle she often came home for weekends. She told mother that my dresses were too long and then shortened them herself. According to my sister, I was just a little girl. At eleven, I desperately wanted to look like my peers, but I gritted my teeth and wore the dresses.

My brother then came home and informed mother that I looked like a freak because all the other girls wore their dresses much longer. So mother let the hems back down. The next time Love came home and wanted to shorten my clothes, I rebelled.

"Whose dresses are these?" I demanded.

The hems remained down.

Driving With Miss. Mull

By serving banquets for the Lions Club, the Elks, and various school functions, Miss. Mull made money to help run the cafeteria. During basketball tournament time she also served meals to visiting teams. Since I was familiar with the facilities, she asked me to help serve. I have vivid memories of one banquet.

We had two wonderful cooks, both named Schoelch whom Miss. Mull usually drove home after a function. This night there were also two other girls and me in the car. The cooks, who were both rather large women, were in the front seat. One of them was having trouble finding a place for her foot until Miss. Mull took her foot off the accelerator for a moment.

Suddenly, we were careening around a corner with Miss. Mull yelling, "Lift your foot, Miss. Schoelch!" Finally Miss. Mull switched off the ignition and we came to rest against a newly planted tree in someone's lawn. After settling with the owner about damages, we finally delivered the other passengers and Miss. Mull and I drove to Homer.

In truth, Miss. Mull was a notoriously bad driver without any help from her passengers, primarily because she was so distracted. Beside running the cafeteria and teaching, she was caring for her elderly parents who were both in ill health.

She seldom had time to apply make up or dress properly. Instead, she used the rear view mirror to apply her makeup, often removing both hands then grabbing the wheel moments before the car left the road. Then she repeated the procedure to adjust her hat before returning the mirror to its proper angle. Anyone driving behind her would have thought she was drunk.

Frances Plays Cupid

Homer wasn't the only stop the train made between Rushville and Shelbyville. Other students got on at Rays Crossing and a career girl from Manilla rode to her job as executive secretary for a firm in Shelbyville each day.

Emma Pence was a beautiful woman about five feet six with an oval face and dark eyes and hair. Her sister, who was an accomplished seamstress, made her clothes which were very tailored and always in fashion.

Doc's basketball coach, Tim Campbell and Emma were dating. Now and then the couple would quarrel. Eventually, after one of these spats, Tim would find me and give me a letter to deliver to Emma. Other times, while I was in study hall, I would see Tim patrolling the aisles. This was my cue to raise my book so he could slip a letter beneath it. The transaction was completed so quickly no one ever caught him.

Once in awhile Emma would be the one to give me a letter. Those mornings Tim would catch me at my locker to ask how Doc was doing so I could make my delivery. All this romantic intrigue certainly enlivened the school routine.

An Old Nemesis Returns

During my sophomore and junior years, Marjorie, the girl who'd skipped a grade at Homer became a problem in my life once again. She'd been attending Manilla High School which didn't offer the courses she needed to a get into Indiana University, so she transferred to Shelbyville for her last two years.

Not a day went by when she didn't call me stupid or put me down in some way because I hadn't been promoted as she had.

She took delight in demeaning me in front of my friends, making those two years pure hell.

One Fall, the girls from Rays Crossing who rode the train, gave a Halloween party. Marjorie insisted that I go. At first I refused, but the girls hosting the party pleaded with me to come. So like the dummy Marjorie insisted I was, I finally agreed.

Next, she asked if I had a costume she could wear. We had two outfits at home to choose from — a clown and a gypsy. Guess which one I wound up wearing.

I found out later that originally only Marjorie had received an invitation (which explained why mine arrived such a short time before the party). But the only way Marjorie's father, whose sister was one of my teachers, would let Marjorie attend was if I went along. So Marjorie and her friends hastily revised the guest list.

Because the party was out of town, we were invited to spend the night with our hostesses. Only after I was there did I learn that the party had been devised as a scheme for Marjorie to meet her boy friend, whom she had been forbidden to see. Of course, in order to keep me from exposing the ruse, no one mentioned that everyone else would be bringing a date.

At school the next Monday, Marjorie's aunt called me up on the carpet for not telling her that the forbidden beau was going to be there. I let her know that I was just as much in the dark about the situation as she and that as far as I knew, Marjorie only saw the boy during the party. Later, I found she'd actually slipped out to meet him again after we'd all gone to bed. As a result, I think that teacher's trust in me was damaged.

A Second Chance At the Footlights

When I was a junior, my class presented a play on an improvised stage in our study hall. I was cast as the mother of a character played by classmate Norm Thurston. Unfortunately, my acting skills hadn't improved much since my second grade appearance. At one point in the play I was supposed to say, "I knit sox and shirts." Alas, what came out was, "I knit shocks and sirts." It brought down the hall in laughter.

At the end of the play I was to put my arms around my son and the makeshift curtain was to close, but the boy in charge of the curtain missed his cue. Finally we walked off the stage, but Norm went one way and I went the other. I'm sure the student audience never forgot two such red-faced actors.

The Editor

Despite the ridicule I endured from Marjorie, I managed to be named editor of the school newspaper during the junior class elections. Perhaps Great-grandfather Hoak's journalism genes filtered down to my generation. In any case, my stint as part of the fourth estate came with its own down side.

When we returned to class a few weeks after the election, we found the entire school in a mess. A group of disgruntled students, angry over what they saw as favoritism toward the elected classmates, had sneaked in over the weekend, turning over hundreds of lockers, scattering the contents throughout the halls.

Ink was poured on notebooks and texts were torn. Sorting the belongings and returning them to the proper owners took all day so classes were suspended until the task was completed.

Although the vandals were identified and suspended for a certain period and their parents were required to reimburse those whose belongings were damaged, the episode did not bode well for my tenure as editor. The sad thing was that the guilty students could have earned an equal chance at success during their high school careers by channeling their energy in the same direction as that of those they considered the favored few.

Producing the paper was an challenging experience. Mr. Linville, our chemistry and physics teacher was the paper's sponsor. He had been gassed in World War I and had a slight facial twitch, but was really an old dear. I had a pretty good staff as well, except for one boy who could never complete his sports articles in time to meet our deadline with the printer. Still, every edition was eventually distributed — until I took our final (and week overdue) issue to the printer.

The printing company, the only one in our area at the time, had just received a major (high income) order that was going to take several weeks to complete. Despite my pleas, they refused to interrupt the process long enough to run such a low-paying job as a high school newspaper.

Although I understood the economics of the situation, I was crying when I returned to face Mr. Linville. He patted my shoulder and said, "Neither you nor your staff is at fault. Years from now you'll view this as a minor disappointment."

I wish I could confirm that his words proved to be true. But I still remember having to explain to the whole school, and the seniors in particular, that the edition that was to contain details of their senior prom and interviews that discussed their hopes for the future was not to be.

The irony of the situation was that the student whose articles were always late pursued a career in journalism, eventually becoming the publisher of a highly regarded daily newspaper. You can bet few of his own reporters ever missed their deadline.

Many years later, my father and I were discussing my high school years and I mentioned the hell I'd suffered at Marjorie's hands because I hadn't passed that fifth grade test. Dad told me that there had actually been five of us who'd passed the exam. Kyle Thrall scored the highest, I was second, Lowene Edwards was third and Marjorie was fourth, but none of the other parents felt that we should skip such a basic grade.

Oh, how I wish I'd learned all that before I had to endure those sophomore and junior years.

Hard Times Meant Doing With Less

The impending depression limited my wardrobe. With two siblings in college at the same time and little money I learned to do without unnecessary things. I had two cotton dresses, two broomstick skirts and two blouses. For winter, Mom made me two blue velveteen blouses and invested in two sets of collars and cuffs that I wore inter-changeably with the velveteen blouses. Part of the clothes were hand-me-downs from Love and Lowene. All the girls were in the same boat, so no one thought anything about seeing me in the same outfits week after week.

Working Our Way Toward a Prom

In order to have a combined prom with the seniors, the junior class held bake sales on the public square and were also given the privilege of selling Cokes, candy, popcorn and Eskimo pies at the basketball games. Only those juniors who made the honor roll were allowed to participate. Each girl carried her tray of items strapped around her neck and were assigned a boy to carry the heavier drink tray.

Cokes and popcorn were passed up to the top seats but foil-wrapped Eskimo pies were thrown to each buyer who then threw their quarters and half-dollars back down to the girls to pay for their purchases. If we received dollar bills they had to be passed down and change returned the same way.

The boy assigned to me was not a very good catcher. Nor was he very proficient at throwing. Having an older brother who had shared his love of baseball proved to be a mixed blessing. I soon found that I was doing all the throwing.

Perhaps because of my close association with Miss. Mull, I was elected chairman of the food committee for the prom. That year's seniors had decided they wanted *real* food instead of punch and cookies. What they got was sandwiches, potato salad, Cokes, and cake and ice cream. Of course, since I was in charge I had to clean up, so my time on the dance floor was very limited. But not being a very good dancer, I had a good time anyway.

Career Choices

In my senior year, I was elected editor of the school's yearbook, the Squib. I was looking forward to the all-state conference that had been scheduled for editors and staff of high school annuals. But that week Love, who was teaching in New Castle, wanted to drive up to Michigan University to visit her fiancee who was interning in the university hospital. Dad wanted me to go along to check out the university for my college career.

I didn't want to go to Michigan. I wanted to go to Purdue, which had a good home economics department, and study to become a dietician. Toward that goal, I'd taken extra classes during high school that focused on food and diet. Despite this, my father didn't think I'd make a good dietician.

In those days hospitals were about the only places that employed dieticians. Industrial and school dining rooms that required dieticians came into being much later. Dad said, "The first time a sick baby whose diet you'd been monitoring died in your arms, you'd go to pieces."

In addition to his bias against my goal, Dad wanted all of us to graduate from his alma mater. Later I learned he'd talked to the principal and the yearbook sponsor who arranged for someone to take my place at the conference. Unfortunately that person didn't bring back much helpful information. She was more interested in writing poetry than being an editor.

Dad couldn't leave his patients so Mother, who didn't drive, went with us. I drove to New Castle where we had supper and Love took the wheel of our rather crowded Ford coupe. Later that night we began encountering patches of fog that soon thickened to challenge that old Ford's headlamps.

Love had just mentioned that she was beginning to tire, when I thought I heard something and yelled, "Stop! Stop right now." Startled by my outburst, Love slammed on the breaks.

Just then there was an ear-splitting blast from a train whistle. The swirling fog thinned for a moment and four feet in front of us sat a massive black engine. Moments later a second train thundered by and the engine in front of us moved on.

Love, shaking from such a close call, gladly relinquished the wheel to me to complete the rest of the trip to Ann Arbor.

Alternative School Transportation

During my senior year, the train to Shelbyville was discontinued. Parents of students commuting from Homer then bought an old Ford so we could drive to school. The twenty miles were a chore when it rained or snowed as the car leaked.

Usually there were freshmen Byron Willis, Fred Mull and Virginia Carr, and eighth grader Wendell Carr and myself. A sophomore, Mildred Maze, was sometimes the sixth.

Wendell's parents were divorced and his father worked nights driving a cattle truck to the Indianapolis stockyards, leaving Wendell and his younger brother alone. They often overslept, which in turn made us late for school. We got a reputation for tardiness and the principal warned us that we couldn't get excused again if we didn't mend our ways. We solved the problem by calling the boys early enough that they could get ready for school.

Much to the principal's delight, we began to arrive on time. Then one morning we came upon Miss. Mull, who had run out of gas. We had just gone through Rays Crossing, so we returned and brought back a five gallon of gas, which one of the boys poured in her tank. Of course, by now we were late.

The others stood behind me as I faced Mr. Loper, our very disgusted principal, who said, "I don't see why you can't get to school on time. Miss. Mull also lives in Homer and she gets here on time. What is your excuse today?"

I looked him straight in the eye and said, "Today Miss. Mull ran out of gas and we drove back to Rays Crossing to get her some."

Mr. Loper threw up his hands and said, "Here are your passes. Now get out of here."

We were late only twice after that. Our Ford was such an old rattletrap of a car that we had to wire something back on almost every night. Once it simply stopped dead in the road. I stayed with the car and the boys walked back to town to get Wendell's father, who also ran the Homer garage, to come and get it running again..

The other time we were late we were driving on snow and ice. We reached an area where there was a deep ravine on one side and a lesser ditch on the other. When the car started skidding toward the ravine, I over-compensated and we wound up in the ditch, but the boys got out and pushed us back onto the road. Byron and Wendell were about six feet tall and Fred was five feet ten, just strong country boys really.

We were all badly shaken. Virginia or Diddy (who'd had previous experience with my driving and ditches) had a small lump on her head from hitting the roof of the car. We sat there for awhile before Byron Willis declared, "Let's go by God!" At that point, I decided if he was so eager, he should do the driving.

The snow continued to fall and often we had to struggle through high drifts. When we reached school, we found that similar drifts had prevented several of the school buses from completing their routes. Many of the kids who lived in town hadn't made it either.

Mr. Loper couldn't believe we'd made it to school. He phoned the Indianapolis radio station and asked them to broadcast that Shelbyville had canceled its classes, then sent us home. The return trip was extremely slow going. Highway plows had cleared the roads here and there but the layer of ice remained.

Keeping Out Possible Intruders

I made another visit to the University of Michigan shortly after my high school graduation. My brother was receiving his degree and Dad's class was holding a reunion. I invited Frances Fisher to go along to keep me company.

We were to stay two nights at Doc's fraternity where only the graduating seniors remained. Somehow Frances and I got the idea that our room might be invaded, so we pushed some furniture in front of the door. We overslept and Dad had a hard time getting into the room to wake us. We were teased about our barricade, but it was a fun time. We watched the graduation exercise and had a small taste of fraternity life.

NINE

TIME TO LEAVE HOME

After I finished high school in the Spring of 1929, Dad could not afford to send me to college. Economic conditions were steadily worsening and jobs were non-existent in rural areas and the surrounding towns.

Dad decided to send me to Detroit to be with Lowene. His hope was that I might find work in a larger city. When I first arrived I studied the want ads and scheduled interviews all over Detroit. Taking street cars and using transfers was a daunting experience for a small town girl and I was soon completely bewildered. It was obvious Lowene would have to come along so I wouldn't get lost before I learned my way around.

One place had no waiting room, so Lowene had to accompany me into the interviewer's office. The personnel director looked down her nose at me and asked if Lowene was going to go with me on all my interviews. Even after I explained that I was new to the city, her attitude remained aloof.

I had hoped to find a filing job since I wasn't really qualified for anything else. Although I was unsuccessful, my first few interviews taught me that my biggest obstacle to employment was going to be my lack of typing skills. In high school I had taken all solid subjects (college prep). Knowing that mastering a typewriter would also come in handy when I began to write term papers in college, I decided it was time to learn.

The personnel director at the library where Lowene was working told me that she would have a position for me if I could get my typing speed up to fifty words a minute. That was the only encouragement I needed. I signed up for a month's worth of typing and spelling classes at a local business school. Then I rented a typewriter and practiced every evening after class.

Such concentrated effort began to pay off and I soon had my speed up to fifty words a minute. The period I'd paid for had not yet run out, so I decided to stay until the course was over.

One boy had been there for quite awhile and he was typing regularly about seventy words a minute. It was clear to everyone in the class that he was also the teacher's pet. After one timed test, the teacher looked directly at her favorite student and asked if any one had typed seventy-five words a minute. Although the boy didn't raise his hand, I did.

The instructor marched over to my desk, ripped my paper out of the typewriter and said, "You must have cheated by starting before the others. You'll have to retake the test."

When I get angry, I concentrate much better. She stood right beside me as I typed, which added to my determination to prove I was not a liar. This time I scored *seventy-nine* words a minute. There was no more talk about my cheating.

The course was almost over, so I decided to take the test at the library. Without the teacher's added pressure pushing me, my speed was only sixty-five words a minute, but I was hired as a clerk-typist in the catalog department. It was a real pleasure to walk in and tell that teacher that I had a position and would not be returning. Still, she had to have the final word. She insisted I'd be sorry if I didn't take more secretarial courses.

Once again, she was wrong.

Winter in Detroit

When I first arrived in Detroit, I had a thin little spring coat. Although I layered my clothing, I nearly froze when that icy wind blew off the Great Lakes. Now that I was working, Dad, who had always stressed investing in quality clothes that would last a long time, suggested I buy a fur coat. Since the depression was raging, I got an expensive muskrat coat for a only a hundred dollars. What a difference it made.

I lived with Lowene for three years, working at the library and saving to help pay my tuition and buy a few clothes. During that time I also took a year each of English and French at Detroit City College, which later became Wayne University.

During the winter Detroit flooded the public tennis courts so residents could ice skate. In my French course I had met a boy named Bill who now invited me to go skating. I was afraid to admit I'd never been on skates. Neither had Lowene, but the Saturday before my date, she and I set out to learn.

I managed to skate around the outside edge, holding to the fence to maintain my balance. But Lowene's ankles were weak and would not hold her up. Suddenly she was sliding on her bottom into the midst of the experienced skaters in the middle of the rink. A big tall skater set her on her feet and shoved her out further into crowd with her arms flailing.

It took a while, but I finally managed to get to her and somehow together we got back to the edge. Lowene had had enough and went in to the hut to stay warm, but I kept at it until I decided I'd learned enough to be able to go out with Bill.

My Irate Library Patron

Sometimes I was sent to the downtown library to fill in at the desk, stamping library cards and finding books for customers. As the Depression wore on into 1931 and 1932, things became very bad for the citizens of Detroit, as well as the rest of the nation. Because there was no money for even small amenities, unemployed men would use the library copies of the newspapers to look for work.

Many were well-educated, older men and were humiliated that they had no job. Others were bums who came in during winter to get warm and remained all day. This branch was in a cosmopolitan area and most of the books they stocked were in other languages. Because the library needed the money, a once free library card now cost twenty-five cents to renew. Many of the non-English speaking patrons who came in to take out books often didn't have even the ten cent fare for a bus or street car.

Manning one of the two main desks in the hall at the entrance to the building was a librarian named Kurt who was noted for speaking seven languages. I was working the second desk across from his. As usual, the security guard was somewhere in the main part of the library, rousting the bums from their sleep to send them on their way, when I encountered what could have become a major problem.

Kurt was stamping books for two patrons and I was waiting on a man of about fifty or sixty. I was trying to explain that his card had expired and that he would have to pay the quarter renewal fee before he could take his books. He began arguing loudly in his native language, which I did not understand, and his expression became quite threatening.

Suddenly, Kurt vaulted over his desk and put himself between me and my patron. I rang the security bell and explained to Kurt what had triggered the man's rage. Kurt began speaking to him in his own language. By the time the guard appeared, things had calmed down somewhat.

After he realized the man had no money to pay for the card, Kurt let him check out the books but retained his card. As the guard escorted the man out of the building, Kurt asked me, "Did you know he had his fist ready to bust you in the jaw?"

I said, "Yes, and I was wondering whether I could move fast enough to dodge it."

That evening the guard saw me out to wait for my bus.

Vacationing on the Lake

One summer Lowene and I took an American-owned boat up through Lake Huron and Lake Superior to Duluth and returned via the British-owned line to Detroit. Lowene suffered terribly from allergies and hay fever and thought a boat trip would be a good way to get away from ragweed and pollen. Unfortunately, the boat was filled with flowers. We could put them outside our cabin and ask that they be removed from our dinner table, but only by retreating on deck could we avoid the bouquets positioned throughout the lounge.

Our first night out when we entered the lounge, several sailors asked me to dance. Since I considered myself a poor dancer, I declined. But these were persistent fellows, so when I saw one of them coming, I'd duck out one lounge door then back in through another with the boys in pursuit. Unfortunately, one of the other passenger's had imbibed a little too much and kept going out for fresh air and returning as well. After a while, with everyone going out and coming in those doors, I began to feel like I was part of a Mack Sennett film.

The second night out I decided to take a shower before dinner. Our stewardess warned me to leave the porthole open to avoid seasickness. Somehow I had the mistaken idea that our porthole opened onto a deck and passers-by might be able to see in, so I failed to heed her advice. Between the rough seas and the steam from the shower I became deathly ill.

When I came out, Lowene walked me around the deck until I was feeling better. Finally, we went in to dinner. I ordered and was beginning to enjoy my dinner when the captain left his big table and scooted his chair over to our little one. One look at me and he recognized my problem.

You might say the captain had a warped sense of humor. He began discussing various meals he'd encountered on ships, especially those consisting of fat pork and other greasy foods. Soon I was back out on deck. I guess he felt a twinge of guilt for he sent a couple of sailors to take my arms and keep me walking and talking until I recovered my sea legs once more.

On the British line coming home there were even fewer young unattached women, so Lowene convinced me we should both accept the sailors' invitations to dance. One fellow was a little too amorous for my taste and I had an even harder time avoiding him than I had the men on the way out.

Lowene, who was a much better dancer, proved to be a very popular partner, especially with the captain. While they were dancing, she mentioned my problem with his amorous crewman. Shortly after that, the sailor was dispatched on an errand that occupied him most of the night.

Potent Potables

During my time at the library I made friends with another typist. One summer Betty asked me to a picnic at her family's cottage on Lake St. Clair. Her boyfriend picked us up after work and had invited a friend for me. Prohibition was in full swing and the friend had brought along some bathtub gin.

We drove to Betty's house so we girls could change into jeans. As soon as we arrived, the boys started drinking, as did Betty. Catching a glimpse of Dad's bottle of medicinal whiskey was as close to liquor as I'd ever come and one little taste did it for me. I poured the rest of the gin down the bathroom sink and refilled my glass with water.

Since we'd not yet eaten, Betty soon became ill as did the friend. Betty's boyfriend quit drinking and began worrying about what her father would do to him if he brought her to the cottage in that condition. He suggested I help her get under the shower to try to sober her up. She remained under there for a long time and when I got her out all she wanted was to go to bed. I helped her in and then told the boys I wished to go home.

I took the boyfriend's keys and he poured his friend into the back seat. After taking the friend home, I drove to my house, windows down and the cold air blowing. When Betty's boyfriend began to revive and I was sure he was sober enough to drive, I returned his keys and he apologized for himself and his friend.

Of course, when I came in so early, Lowene wanted to know what had happened. She thought I'd handled the situation quite well under the circumstances. Later, Betty felt terrible about the whole mess, but we never rescheduled the picnic.

Riding the Bus

You can see many unusual things when you ride a bus to work each day. I once witnessed a woman go into an epileptic seizure. Another passenger quickly realized what was happening and had the presence of mind to place a pencil between her teeth to prevent her from biting her tongue. He then helped her off the bus and saw her to her home.

Detroit's transportation system included several double-decked buses that had been imported from England. Riding on the upper level provided a wonderful view of what was going on around you. Sometimes you saw more than you wanted.

Although Eliot Ness had succeeded in stopping Al Capone's regime in Chicago, Detroit was still battling gangsters in the early 1930s. Lowene and I were on the top deck of a bus that was about to go beneath an overpass one evening when suddenly we were surrounded by police cars, their lights flashing and sirens blasting. Officers began leaning out windows and firing at the tires of a big black touring car in the lane beside us.

A police bullet went astray and pierced a tire on our bus. The echo of the exploding tire bounced off the walls of the overpass so loudly that everyone on the bus thought we'd been hit and fell to the floor. Most of the police cars raced after the gangsters, but as the bus pulled to the curb, one officer stopped to assure our driver that someone would call for another vehicle.

Other buses kept passing us but were filled to capacity, so we wound up getting home over an hour late. At least the topic of conversation at dinner that evening was lively.

The Gangster Chronicle Continues

As if finding ourselves in the midst of a gun battle wasn't excitement enough, we had yet another encounter with underworld figures. Some time after the bus incident, a gangster was killed in a Detroit hotel. To our dismay, we discovered the man had a home around the corner from our apartment building.

The deceased was laid out in his living room and I think every mobster and most of the curiosity seekers in Detroit came to view the body. We arrived home from work that evening to find a line of people snaking all the way down our block and around the corner. When we tried to get to our apartment, everyone thought we were bucking the line. Finally someone listened to what we were saying and let us through. It was the wee hours of the morning before the crowd disappeared completely.

Making Friends With the Local Grocer

In addition to a resident mobster, also down the street from our apartment was a little grocery that specialized in fruits and vegetables. Lowene and I often visited early in the morning and discovered that the immigrant owner (a Hungarian, I think) had a son at Michigan. After learning of our own connections to the school, he was soon treating us like valued customers.

When we reached for tomatoes or peaches or some other fresh item, he'd wave us away from the open bins and say, "No, no. I get for you," then disappear into the back. One day some other women from the neighborhood complained that he'd gotten us fresher fruit. He looked at them and said, "*They* (pointing at us) do not squeeze and bruise the fruit as you do. I will not give *them* picked over fruit."

A Welcome Break

Once brother-in-law Gifford came to Detroit to attend a conference. After his meeting he gave his hard-working sisters-in-law a rare treat by taking us to the Ziegfeld Follies. The costumes were fabulous, the women gorgeous and the music unforgettable.

Then, just before I was to leave for college, Gifford came to take us to the ballet. I wanted to go, but had a bad cold and was quite ill. Dr. Gifford took charge, checked my temperature and found it was 104°. He gave me aspirin and increased my fluids. Then he and Lowene went to the ballet while I drowned my disappointment in orange juice and ginger ale.

A Stressful College Orientation

Because of Dad's opposition, I'd rethought my plan to be a dietitian, which required a heavy concentration in science and mathematics, neither of which I excelled in nor enjoyed. In addition, working in the library had reawakened a passion for books and reading that had been subjugated by the demanding college preparatory classes of my high school years.

The seeds of my love for books had been planted by Lowene years earlier when she'd taken such delight in reading aloud to me on those enchanting afternoons on our front porch in Homer. That and my recent work experience pointed the way to the perfect career. Like Lowene, I would become a librarian.

When I told my university advisor of my choice, he confessed that I was the first student he'd counseled in that area before. "Librarians have to know a little bit about everything, so I guess you should branch out into all subjects."

So that's what I did. My naivete in trusting such vague advice would later return to haunt me.

In addition to my transcripts from Detroit City College and talking to an advisor, the university required a physical exam before admssion. I was still carrying a low-grade fever from the cold that had canceled my ballet trip, so the doctor ordered a chest X-ray. The spot he found on one of my lungs indicated I'd been battling pneumonia. In those pre-antibiotic days the only prescription was more rest, not an easy thing for an in-coming college freshman.

One section of the medical questionnaire also asked for data on my menstrual cycle. Mine had always been very irregular and it had been four months since my last one. Whether the doctor was alarmed or simply suspicious that I'd lied about being chaste, I'm not sure. In any case, the situation resulted in my first pelvic exam at the age of twenty-two. Although that doctor detected no serious problems, later ones would.

By the time the physical finished I was exhausted. My brother, who taught health, had instructed me on proper posture, so when they'd asked me to stand correctly I'd done so. But immediately after that I slumped. As they were debating what grade to give me, I said, "If you'd been through what I have today, you'd slump too." Since I'd demonstrated I knew how to stand properly, they finally gave me an A minus.

Financial Matters

Because Dad had promised to help with my college expenses, I listed my parents' house as my home address when I registered for classes. Annual tuition for out-of-state students was three hundred dollars. I'd managed to save enough for my books and clothes and my first semester's room and board as well as a hundred and fifty dollars toward the tuition.

Around this time, Wendell Wilkie, who later ran for president, bought a farm across the road from one of Dad's. A little creek ran through both properties which were separated by a little bridge. Wilkie decided to import young beef from Mexico, fatten them on his farm, and then sell them. Unfortunately one of his bulls tore down the fence beneath the bridge and got to ten head of Dad's registered Aberdeen Angus cows.

Unknown to our neighbor, his Mexican cattle were carrying anthrax, which the bull transmitted to Dad's stock. He had to kill the ten cows, burn the grass, and turn the sod over and spray it with chemicals. The process had to be repeated several times before the ground finally tested clear and could be used for stock. Luckily the rest of Dad's herd was pastured elsewhere and did not come down with the disease. Still, the economic cost added to Dad's problems.

When the second semester expenses came due, he sent enough to cover my room and board, but all I had to put toward tuition was fifty dollars and Dad's promise to send the remaining hundred after he sold some hogs. Unfortunately, that event had to wait until the hogs were heavy enough to sell.

As a result of the delay, I was called up on the carpet by the university's treasurer every week until Dad was able to send the money. Soon after that, I learned that my three years with Lowene could have qualified me for in-state tuition of only a hundred dollars a year. The next year I took advantage of that.

In addition to what I'd saved, Lowene and Doc (who was teaching) loaned me money for college at various times. Because of the Depression, the city of Detroit was broke, so the library was paying Lowene a combination of cash and what was known as script. (A provisional certificate much like an IOU issued by an entity such as a municipality and backed by shares in property such as government buildings. As the Depression began to lift, issuers of script retired the certificates much as they would a bond issue today.)

I'd used some of Lowene's script to pay my dorm rent. The university was trying to complete construction of two new dorms and had recently discovered that Detroit's Hudson Department Store accepted script in payment for merchandise such as beds, dressers and desks. The treasurer began to hound me for more script. Eventually Detroit got back on its feet, but in the meantime I had furnished several rooms in those new dorms.

Back to the University Hospital

At Christmas freshman were in charge of decorating the dorm's common areas. We each had to furnish an ornament for the tree, which was so tall that a step ladder was required to reach the higher branches. To decorate the doors and the fireplace mantle, we decided to hang pine boughs and big red ribbon bows.

My arms and hands were full of greenery when the dorm director insisted I hold something for her, so I put a bough in my mouth to free one hand. Later that evening I began to itch. By morning I has a rash on my chest, back, arms and face. The Dorm director took one look and sent me to the university clinic.

When I entered, no one was around. Every chair but one was covered with sheets so naturally I sat in the undraped one. Suddenly a young woman came in and cried, "Why did you sit in that chair? Now I have to scrub it again." As I jumped up, a young doctor came in and led me to an examining room. Two young interns joined us and a diagnostic discussion ensued. One said scarlet fever. One said measles. The other said scarlatina.

Finally, the doctor took me down the hall saying, "The women's ward is full. Where am I going to put you?" We were passing the men's ward at that moment and several voices sang out, "Put her in here, Doc."

He left me in an isolation room to wait for Dr. Jiminez, the physician in charge of contagious diseases. Even after *he* examined me, no one seemed to know what was wrong. So I was given permission to place a reverse charges call to my father.

After listening to my description of my symptoms, Dad asked, "What did you do yesterday?" I told him about trimming the dorm. "Did you put a bough in your mouth?" he wanted to know.

When I said yes, he asked for the doctor's name and then said he wanted to talk to him. I sent someone to find Dr. Jiminez and explain that his patient's father wished to speak to him.

I heard Dr. Jiminez say, "Foxy Grandpa, is that you?" and after much laughter, he handed the phone back to me. Dad said, "You're allergic to pine. From now on stay away from it."

A very amused Dr. Jiminez told me that Dad had asked, "Jiminez, haven't you learned to identify allergies, yet?" It seems they had been in medical school together.

Thanks to Dad's suggested treatment, I received the biggest dose of caster oil I ever had. It tasted terrible, but it cured me pronto.

TEN

SOCIAL LIFE ON CAMPUS

Dad had told me that the Army vs Michigan football game would be exciting and colorful and urged me to attend. I wasn't, and still am not, fond of football, but I went. It *was* colorful with the big yellow mums and blue ribbons and banners and a home crowd dressed in similar hues. But the alumni were out in full force, most of them drunk and staggering or sick.

Michigan won, but it was extremely cold and I was freezing. When Dad asked me how I'd liked it, I told him it had been colorful, but not so exciting. I never attended another game.

The two year old dormitory to which I had been assigned, was located between the university hospital and a cemetery. When you gave a date the name of the dorm where they were to pick you up, they always asked, "Are you in the sick end or the dead end?"

My dorm roommate was a sophomore who had asked to be put with her previous roommate but had been assigned a freshman as a little sister. We got along fine, but she spent all her free time in her ex-roommate's room. When that girl's little sister flunked out, my roommate was given permission to move. For the rest of the semester I was on my own and very lonely.

Sorority Life

I was rushed by several sororities and pledged my favorite, Alpha Xi Delta. The Alpha Xi Delta girls were fun and helped me to overcome my loneliness at the dorm.

The night of my initiation my sorority sisters fixed me up with a blind date. Carlyle Rogers was a local boy, a good friend of all the members. He had dated many of them and often helped out when an escort was needed. His fiancee, his high school sweetheart, was teaching in New York state.

Because of the Depression and Carlyle's need to obtain his teaching degree, the couple had postponed their marriage. They'd decided that occasional casual dates with varied partners would keep them from being too lonely, as long as neither of them became too friendly with any particular person. For our blind date we went to a movie and stopped for a Coke.

A nickel Coke and a dime movie (often Dutch-treat) were the highpoint of most student's lives during the Depression era. Most couples opted for study dates at the campus library or, if during the day, strolls around the Arboretum.

For my sophomore year I moved into the sorority house where I had two roommates, Charlotte Anderson from Manchester, New Hampshire and Ruth Hoefer from Oshkosh, Wisconsin. We shared a study room with a big walk-in closet for our clothes, but slept in a large third-floor dormitory with everyone else.

The dorm's cleaning lady took advantage of the especially warm Fall we were having and opened the unscreened windows in the sleeping area to air the mattresses and bedding. We left them open at night to cool the room. One evening Charlotte and I had been studying late and went to bed long after the others. We'd just settled down when we felt something swish over our heads.

I whispered, "Char, is that what I think it is?" She said, "Yes, it's a bat. Maybe it'll fly away."

We covered our heads with our sheets and kept our fingers crossed. But it wasn't long until the others awakened and all bedlam let loose. Someone slipped downstairs and got brooms and mops and towels. Once we each had a weapon, we turned on the light and twenty scantily-dressed girls went after that bat.

Someone yelled, "Here he is over here!" then someone else cried out, "No, he's over here!" as we kept trying to herd the poor bat toward the window. Our yells and screams continued until suddenly the bat decided he'd had enough and darted through the window. Immediately, we heard the cheers of an all-male chorus.

We looked out to see the entire membership of the Sigma Nu fraternity perched on the eight foot brick wall that separated our houses. Several called out, "Need any help, girls? We'd be glad to assist you." We called back, "No, thanks, we took care of the problem."

Suddenly it dawned on us that skimpy night clothes were not proper attire for co-ed conversation, especially when back-lit by inside lighting. Out went the lights. After a few groans from the brothers who'd been enjoying the show, silence reigned once more.

Chivalry on a Snowy Evening

Carlyle asked me to a dance at the Women's League. We drove his car, which he'd named Mary because she was often contrary. The evening was cool, but during the four hour dance a blizzard struck Ann Arbor. When we came out, drifts, some of them six feet high, covered the streets and sidewalks.

Mary took us just so far before getting stuck in a drift. We started hoofing it in our tux and gown. I was wearing my fur coat, but no boots, just dress shoes. The last few yards of our trek, Carlyle was almost carrying me. At the sorority, our house mother was serving hot chocolate to warm up all the escorts who'd been forced to seek refuge.

My platonic relationship with Carlyle provided many happy moments during my early college years. When he and his long-time fiancee were finally married, I was unable to attend, but sent a gift and my best wishes for their happiness.

Music, Maestro, Please

Dances were a favorite activity on campus. Big name bands often played for our proms. The depression hit these musicians especially hard. Sometimes they played for very little money, just a meal and enough to buy gas for the old school buses they drove. Often, if their engagements were far apart, they had to hock their instruments to survive. University proms were a highlight because they meant real money.

At various times during my university years I danced to the Dorsey Brothers, Jan Garber, Jimmy Lunceford, Kay Kaiser, Wayne King, and Red Nichols and his Five Bad Pennies.

Red and his band offered more than dance music, including funny songs so you listened rather than danced. Once when Red played, the band broke off at ten o'clock to broadcast over the radio. The technical aspects of broadcasting muted the music inside the hall, so everyone went outside, turned on the radio station and danced on the patio until the show ended and we could enjoy the real thing once again.

A Moment's Error in Judgment

Hoping to graduate sooner, I took a course or two during summer breaks. Love's landlady, who worked at the university library, helped me get a job there.

One summer day I joined my friend Helen and one of her sorority's pledges for lunch at the Women's League cafeteria. The pledge lived in northern Michigan and her father was a doctor, so we had a lot in common and the noon hour passed pleasantly.

Several days after our lunch, the police paid me a visit. They asked if I'd written three hundred dollars worth of checks which had been returned to a local department store for insufficient funds. When I assured them I hadn't, they asked me to write my name over and over. I complied, but because I was upset, my hand was shaking.

One of the men, a handwriting expert, finally agreed that my signature did not match the one on the hot checks. At that point, I remembered that during my luncheon with Helen and the pledge, I'd left the table to get another glass of tea while Helen went for napkins. And I'd left my purse on the table. When I looked in my checkbook, several checks were missing.

Later that day Dad called to warn me not to be frightened if the police came to see me. I told him he was a little late. Dad and I kept very little in the account in question, depositing just enough to pay my rent and school expenses as they came due. Dad immediately canceled the account and opened a new one.

I later learned the pledge had been about to flunk out of school and had moved in with three boys, using my stolen checks to furnish their apartment. Once the department store and the police contacted her father, he made the purchases good and took his wayward daughter home.

Later that summer Helen, who'd been quite upset by what had happened, asked me to join her on a blind date with her boyfriend who was an intern and his friend who was also studying medicine. My date's name was Patrick Haas. He told me he wanted to meet me because we had both been victims of the sorority pledge. Patrick had been dating her when she abruptly dumped him for one of the boys in the apartment.

Frances the Guinea Pig

Patrick was learning to write up patient histories by creating imaginary cases. When I had an attack of appendicitis and had to go to the university clinic later that summer, he was delighted to be able to visit me and practice on a real person.

Much to the embarrassment of my clinic roommate, a redhead who was being treated for severe sunburn, Patrick asked probing questions about both my medical history and my current condition. Unfortunately, there was no screen or curtain between the beds that we could pull to give us privacy.

My open answers to Patrick's queries surprised him. But as a doctor's daughter, I was used to hearing such personal questions and answered without feeling self-conscious.

A Tragedy in Love's Family

One summer day I had a very strange visit at the library from Gifford's brother Allen (a slightly older version of my shadow from the day of the wedding.) He seemed very agitated and asked if I could go somewhere to talk. I was working and couldn't leave, but offered to see him when I got off. That didn't seem to suit him and after a moment he left. He was only about sixteen or seventeen at the time, and I learned later that Gifford was unaware that his younger sibling had even been in town.

Not long after that visit, Allen's parents, who had moved to Kalamazoo, reported that he was missing and had perhaps been kidnaped. His body was later found in a wooded area near their old home in New Jersey. As far as I know, the mystery of his death was never solved, but the episode at the library has always haunted me. *(Note: A 2014 internet search indicates Allen may have taken his own life sometime around 1935-36)*

The Ultimate Blind Date

The summer before I began my junior year, a sorority sister named Sue called to ask me to accept a blind date. I had just come in from my library job and was very tired. Since I'd planned a quiet evening, I declined. But Sue insisted, saying, "His name's Colin Macdonald and he'll be there around eight." Then she hung up before I could protest further.

After scrounging something to eat, I took a quick shower and slipped on a robe. As I was heading for my room, I heard someone playing the piano in the sorority's parlor. I called out to verify that the pianist was my date and told him I'd be down in a moment.

Colin and I walked to a hangout for college students, an ice cream parlor, where we drank Cokes and danced to the juke box. We also talked about our families. He told me that his branch of the Macdonalds had emigrated from Scotland in the mid 1800s and recounted the family legend about the origin of the variant spelling of their last name.

It seems that long ago it was the custom of the clan to select as chief a man who won a feat of physical superiority. In this particular case, the eligible contestants were to row across a loch (lake) to an island. Whoever touched land first would thus become the clan's new chief.

According to family lore, when Colin's direct ancestor saw he was not going to win, he drew his saber, cut off his hand and threw it onto the island. His relatives' contention that he had indeed *touched* land first resulted in a family feud. From that point on, to distinguish their line from that of others in the MacDonald clan, Colin's ancestors spelled their name with a small <u>d</u>.

Although there's no way to verify the tale, it certainly made an interesting story, especially for a first date.

When we were ready to go home, Colin discovered he'd left his wallet back at his fraternity. Fortunately, I had enough money with me to pay our bill. I teased him that having to repay his debt was a novel way to insure a second date.

Entertainment on campus was sparse in the summertime, but once in awhile the Women's League or the student union brought in a band. Thus Colin was able to pay me back by taking me dancing. He was a very good dancer and, although he was six feet to my own five foot four, with my two inch high heels we meshed very well. We dated on and off the rest of my time in college.

Bad Advice Sets a Precedent

When the second semester of my Junior year rolled around, I was called into to the Dean's office. He informed me that I had two minors, but there was no way I could earn enough credits in any one subject for a major unless I attended a fifth year of college.

I explained about my sponsor, who had instructed me to take a variety of subjects, as he assumed a librarian should be knowledgeable in everything. Although I was trembling, I told the Dean, "I think you should be able to find a way for me to graduate at the proper time."

To my surprise and delight, I was eventually notified that my current courses qualified me for something called a *Pre-Library Science* major. Many years later during my library career in Indiana, the head of my division hired a girl from the Michigan Library School. When I asked her what her major was, she answered, *Pre-Library Science*. It seems my situation had established an enduring curriculum.

Mystery Dinners

For my last year at Michigan my roommates and I moved to an apartment where we were able to cook our own meals. Dad had paid to have some of our vegetables and fruits canned at the Homer canning factory and contributed several cases to our larder.

To save money, he'd instructed that no labels be attached to the cans. Since the packing boxes were labeled, this shouldn't have been a problem. But when I came home from class, I found that my roommates had stacked the individual cans on the shelf. I asked if they'd been arranged in some way that would let us know what we were getting.

Their startled expressions told me they hadn't. We ate quite well that semester, although we never knew what we'd be having for dinner until we opened a can.

ELEVEN

POST UNIVERSITY LIFE

I graduated from Michigan at mid-term and was offered a temporary position in the catalog department of the Detroit public library, filling in for a girl who was ill. Once again I moved in with Lowene. I'd made up my mind that I wanted to be a children's librarian and planned to go to Western Reserve University in Cleveland for the specialized courses in that area which Michigan did not offer.

When I got to Cleveland that fall, I found a room - really a converted sun porch - in a home on Euclid Avenue managed by a Mr. & Mrs. Snodgrass. The following weekend I went downtown with a group of other library students. We visited a tea room and for fun had our palms and tea leaves read by a gypsy woman.

When she got to my hand, she told me that the letter M played an important part in my life. She said, "You have been living in Michigan and your career will start in Michigan. You will also marry a man whose name begins with the letter M and have two children. Your life line is very long, but your heart line is very short."

None of the others felt their fortunes even came close, but I was stunned that a gypsy in Cleveland knew of my Michigan connection. Many years later I was to look back on the rest of her predictions with equal amazement.

A Special Friendship

After a few days in my children's library courses, I realized that the instructor and I were having a clash of personalities and would never be able to get along. I dropped that class asked the dean to transfer me to one on cataloging. He was delighted to oblige because few students were interested in that area. Since I already had experience in that field, he also felt I would have a better chance of getting work.

My instructor there was Miss Barden and I loved her.

Also in that class was a man named Jim who'd been teaching but wanted to get away from disciplining students. As a teacher he looked at things from the side of a school librarian. As a public or university librarian I viewed our field in a slightly different light. Miss Barden said our lively discussions on how particular books should be cataloged kept the class on its toes.

Jim and I often worked on our cataloging problems together and once or twice we met each other at the movies. Instead of Frances, he called me Frankie.

One day I went over to his desk to discuss one of the books on our list. We argued a little about the right catalog selection and then he suddenly asked, "You know I'm a lay brother, a teaching priest, don't you?"

My religious exposure had been rather limited so I said, "No, I know nothing about the Catholic Church and I have no Catholic friends, but what does it matter?"

He explained that every Catholic family designated one child to become a priest or a nun if possible. In his family, he was the one chosen. He talked about the many hardships imposed on those who took their vows, such as the hours spent praying on his knees, and then said, "I've hung up my coat twice and each time my family and the priests have talked me back into the priesthood. Now I'm a lay brother hoping to be a school librarian."

He said he had a job waiting for him and asked me to write him when I, too, found a job. I learned that the only way I could get a letter to him was through a gift. After he finished his classes, we corresponded for a couple of years. Usually I sent my letters along with a gift of handkerchiefs.

Much later I received a prayer card in a letter from someone who said Jim had asked him to destroy my letters if anything ever happened to him. He'd remained a lay brother to please his family but died of a heart attack while still quite young.

Life in Cleveland

In 1936, Cleveland was quite a cosmopolitan city. As the more affluent moved to the suburbs, Euclid Ave. and surrounding areas became a transient place. When cold weather came, my landlords found that the furnace did not work properly. A church group actually owned the house, but they refused to make the necessary repairs and I nearly froze on that sun porch.

Eventually, the Snodgrasses moved to a different house and I moved with them. My room in their new place was large and very warm and cheerful. I now had lots of closet space, a large desk and a comfortable bed.

Several weeks later on a Saturday I heard lots of shouting. When I looked out the window, I saw a woman carrying a big cleaver chasing a man down the street. I wondered what kind of an area I had moved to but was too busy to worry much about it. Still, I was a bit concerned when Mr. Snodgrass began waiting for me at my street car stop every night.

During Spring break in 1937 Patrick Haas came to visit me. He wanted to get married, but I wasn't ready for marriage. I had to finish my library science course, find a job, and then repay my school debt to my family. Soon after I turned him down, he wrote that he had married a nurse. I think I knew he was really just looking for someone to help put him through med school.

A few weeks after Patrick proposed, Colin also came to Cleveland to visit. He was working in Detroit for Ernst and Ernst, an accounting firm, as a summer intern in preparation for completing his degree and becoming a CPA. We spent a nice weekend visiting the sights in Cleveland, but quarreled before he left. Like Patrick, Colin wanted to get married.

Dad's proposal when we each began college was that the older children would help the younger and be paid back after we all became productive. When I insisted I couldn't consider his proposal until I'd repaid my siblings, Colin didn't understand.

Although his own parents were divorced, Colin's father had paid many of Colin's expenses and did not expect to be repaid. Colin could not believe that Dad and Love and Lowene and Doc would hold me to such an agreement. Eventually we smoothed things over and I agreed to reconsider his proposal after we were both earning our own way.

When he left, Mrs. Snodgrass voiced her opinion that she thought Colin was the superior of my two suitors. I told her I thought so too.

An Awkward Situation

In addition to me, the Snodgrasses had also moved their second renter, a man, to their new address. But shortly after that, he moved out and they let the room to a young woman. I was so busy with school work at the time that I didn't meet the new renter. The following Saturday morning there was a knock on my door and a note was slipped under it that read: *Please stay in your room until we knock on your door again.*

A little later there was a big commotion in the hall. The knock on my door came shortly after that and Mrs. Snodgrass explained that the new girl had been entertaining gentlemen in her room several times a night. This lady of the evening and her possessions has been escorted by the police out of the house.

One weekend the Snodgrasses were going to visit a son and Mrs. Snodgrass suggested I invite some of my friends in for supper. Six of us had a wonderful time roasting hot dogs and marshmallows in the Snodgrasses' fireplace.

Unfortunately, a student had recently been raped on her way to her off-campus housing. To prevent anyone else from being attacked, women who stayed late on campus to study were now being sent home with a priest or lay brother as an escort.

When one of my guests mentioned our fun evening and told Dean Hirshberg where I was living, he became very concerned about my situation. He found a girl named Catherine willing to share her on-campus apartment and insisted that I move, even going so far as to get the Snodgrasses to release me from my contract.

I lived in relative peace with my new roommate until shortly before graduation when we had a misunderstanding because I had invited another girl to the apartment to study without asking Catherine's permission. As a result, when Mother came to surprise me for my graduation, things really fell apart.

Catherine had been planning a graduation party. Mother had not thought to make a hotel reservation and now found that there were no available rooms. Not only was it graduation but two big conventions were in town, so Mother had to stay at the apartment.

The situation was a mess. Catherine knew my mother wouldn't approved of the drinks she planned to serve. She told me in no uncertain terms to get rid of my mother. Mother overheard our conversation, but didn't really understand what the problem was. She offered to stay in my room so she would not spoil our fun.

Since I'd helped buy the food and clean the apartment, I was furious with Catherine. After greeting everyone, I joined Mom in the bedroom and let Catherine have the rest of the apartment to entertain her friends. Thankfully, she was moving on after graduation, leaving me in the apartment by myself until I found a permanent job.

Good Times and Bad

After graduation many graduates had a hard time finding work that paid enough to live on. Most positions offered only seventy-five dollars a month. Because of my previous library experience, Dean Hirshberg refused to write me references for such low paying jobs. I began to think I never would get a chance for an interview.

Finally, he hired me himself as a secretary and assistant for a hundred dollars a month. Near the end of July, I received an interview offer for the same salary from Michigan State College. During my interview, the library's director said, "You won't like it here. It's a cow college."

I replied, "I guess I could catalog books for agricultural students as well as any other. After all, I'm a small town girl and worked on my dad's farm." I don't know whether it was because of my response to the director or whether it was the lack of catalogers, but I got the job.

Unfortunately, I had just started working when I became quite ill with abdominal pains. When it was determined that the cause was an ovarian cyst, I went home to Dad. He immediately took me to Dr. Gatch in Indianapolis for surgery.

Like Lowene, I was suddenly facing the possible loss of my ability to have a child. Even a slim chance at someday becoming pregnant seemed better than the certainty of childlessness. I begged my father and Dr. Gatch to save some part of my reproductive organs to at least give me that chance.

When it was all over, Dad explained that the growth had turned out to be my undeveloped twin. Something had gone wrong early in mother's pregnancy. This second fetus stopped developing and attached itself to my ovaries, where it remained as a calcified growth until my own sexual development triggered the problems that had always made my monthly periods so irregular and painful. According to Dad, the inch and a half long cyst was horrible looking, complete with twisted humanoid features.

In answer to my questions concerning my ability to bear children, Dr. Gatch had to admit he didn't know. To remove the cyst, he'd been forced to take all of one ovary and a portion of the other. Shaking his head, he ventured that conceiving a child and carrying it to term might require a miracle.

I would not be allowed to return to work for several weeks, so Dr. Gatch suggested I join Lowene and Doc on a planned trip to Cape Cod where I could sun bathe and swim and complete my recovery. By the time we returned, I was eager to return to work at the Michigan State library.

Remembering my last experience with renting off-campus, I found a room with a faculty member and his wife. Their other tenant was Helen Larrimore, a home economic agent for the State of Michigan. Helen, was dating and later married a co-worker, Elmer Scheidenhelm, a widower with a young son, Alden.

War on the Horizon

In August of 1939, Lowene and Doc and Mother and I drove east for another vacation. We traveled on through New York and up into New Hampshire and Vermont, then took a ferry across Lake Champlain into Canada. One small town where we spent the night was having a Scottish Festival.

As I watched the men in tartan kilts, I was reminded of Colin's story about the rowing contest for chief of his clan. Although Colin and I hadn't seen each other since our meeting in Cleveland two years before, we'd continued to exchange Christmas cards. Since nothing he'd written mentioned his proposal, I feared the door to that part of my life had been closed.

We found the highland music played on bagpipes very interesting, that is, we did until our exhausted party retired. In the wee hours of the night bagpipes sound much less musical.

Doc, who was filming our trip to show his history and geography students, wanted to get some movies of copper and silver mines, but at the place we stopped, we were confronted by a sign that read NO VISITORS. Thinking the mine was simply closed because it was Saturday, Doc climbed over the fence.

A few yards inside the fence he was stopped by an armed guard. As strange as it seems, the two recognized one another as fraternity brothers. The guard explained that because of the escalating tensions between England and Germany, Canada's mines were being patrolled. Although Doc explained the purpose of his visit, he was only allowed to film shots outside the mine.

The encounter was a sobering reminder that, although the economy in the U.S. was slowly rebounding, things looked much less promising in the rest of the world. Within days of our return, England and France were at war with Germany.

TWELVE

A REKINDLED LOVE

Colin had written in one of his Christmas notes that he wished we could see one another again, so the next time there was a campus dance, I asked him to be my escort. As a result, once again we began courting. On weekends, he would drive from Detroit where he was working for an accountant and stay with a friend who was living in Lansing.

During our previous time together, I realized that Colin was a very unhappy and lonely person. His family was the exact reverse of my own. Colin was the oldest, followed by a sister and two younger brothers. But whereas I had been part of a loving family unit, his had been ripped apart when his mother Ruth had divorced Edward, his father, and taken her children from Michigan to Portland, Oregon where her brother was living.

At the time of the divorce, both Ruth and Edward told eleven-year-old Colin that he was now the man of the house and was to take care of his brothers and sister. With all that responsibility on his shoulders, he became a very serious young boy. He got all kinds of jobs to help out. His father, who was a successful attorney, paid support, but his visits were infrequent and he eventually remarried.

Colin's life had also been plagued by illness. As a very young boy he had scarlet fever. The high fever which accompanied the disease slowed his thinking process somewhat, but he had a phenomenal, almost photographic, memory which helped him overcome the problem. Once he mastered something, he never forgot it.

After a bout of pneumonia when Colin was about thirteen, his doctor recommended an outdoor life to build up his stamina. Ruth's interpretation of this was for her oldest son to get a paper route. Rather than strengthening him, delivering papers in Oregon's cold, wet winters produced the opposite result.

Next, Ruth send Colin to YMCA summer camp near Mt. St. Helens where he began to thrive. He was such a serious young man that he soon became a junior counselor and later a senior counselor and a life guard and continued to work at the camp throughout his college years.

As a memento of those wonderful summers, Colin put together several photo albums of the camps and the people he worked with and counseled. Included are several pictures of an extremely thin Colin in swim trunks, each rib clearly showing.

During our courtship, he talked a lot about the young boys he was in charge of at those camps. Many were homesick. By remembering similar emotions that followed his move to Oregon, Colin would hold them and tease them and try to give them the love and attention that had been missing in his own life as a child.

He took his charges on mountain climbing expeditions, but was very careful to remain on well-marked trails and take the terrain slow and easy. Then, on his days off he went to another location with a guide and other adults and tackled tougher peaks.

When Colin was ready for college, his mother sent him back to Michigan with very few clothes, saying, "Let your father outfit you." Edward felt his generous support payments should have been sufficient. He sent Colin out to buy what he needed, but then complained that his son had spent too much money.

Torn between his mother and father, Colin once again experienced deep unhappiness. By the time we met, all he wanted was someone of his own to love who would love him back. Hence his urgency to marry before I felt ready.

Of course, Colin's childhood was not all sadness. He had a mischievous sense of fun. When he was about eight or nine, he decided he wanted to make a go-cart but he needed some wheels. His sister Jean's doll buggy offered the perfect equipment. His strategy to obtain the wheels was to tell Jean how much fun she would have on the go-cart when it was built.

Naturally Colin and his younger brother Dave had all the fun. Jean didn't get many rides. It wasn't long before the buggy was once again able to roll and the go-cart ceased to function.

Colin was also given piano lessons as a child. He was taught to play in chords and didn't read music as well as he should, but he was able to play many popular tunes by ear. In addition, he was an excellent dancer and especially loved to tango.

A Second Chance

After we renewed our interrupted courtship, Colin once again proposed. He knew that I was still paying back my college debt, but assured me he had no objection to my continuing to work and pay my family after we were married. I felt much better about my life at this point and I knew I loved him, so I made both of us happy by saying yes. He bought me a lovely diamond engagement ring and we began to plan our future.

Colin's career was moving up as well. He was working as an accountant with a Mr. Livermore in Detroit. Since Colin was very successful at bringing in new clients, Mr. Livermore made him a partner soon after we were married. Our wedding was held on October 18, 1941 in the chapel of the People's Church on the campus of Michigan State.

We had a small ceremony with Lowene as my only attendant. Colin asked Doc to be his best man. Father Macdonald was ill and unable to attend, as was Colin's mother because of the distance, but both sent their blessings. None of his siblings made it, but my entire family was present - Mother and Dad, Love and Gifford and their two children, as well as Doc's wife Hanne.

I'd planned the wedding myself, but was pleased when a chorus comprised of the local members of my sorority surprised us with a special song during the ceremony. It was a lovely idea and a beautiful moment.

Colin had asked me to smile when I came down the aisle. My Dad gave me away and I told him he would have to support me for I was shaking so bad. He grinned and said, "I was planning on you to hold me up!" I immediately visualized me holding up a two hundred pound man and had a big smile on my face when I walked down the aisle to meet my beloved.

I wore a blush-colored satin gown and Love's veil and carried a bouquet of white roses with a lavender orchid in its center. The orchid was detachable and I wore it on our wedding trip, which was a dead giveaway to everyone that we were a honeymoon couple. Lowene wore a moss green dress and carried a bouquet of yellow and orange mums. Cousin Paul Wiant performed the ceremony.

Traveling to Extremes

Our suitcases were at the inn where we had all stayed the night before and they had been filled with rice. We had returned to change our clothes and as we ran to the car we were also peppered with rice. Love's children, Harold and Nancy had tied old shoes and signs onto our car. We drove a short way, removed all the attachments and then we drove to the duplex that we had been furnishing. It was an upper and as we climbed the stairs we could hear the rice pinging the steps.

Mother and Dad were staying in our place that night, and I worried that the rice might make them slip. So for my first domestic chore as a married woman, I took a whisk broom and swept every step. We put a sign on the door warning Mom and Dad to be careful going up the stairs. We'd packed one suitcase before going to East Lansing but also had to take the ones that contained all the rice.

Although Colin loved mountains, he'd never seen the Smokies, so that's where we were going. We spent the night in Cleveland and started out the next morning. Colin drove until almost dark and then let me take over. I could see lights of a town in the distance but they never seemed to get any nearer. I also noticed that, because of some construction, the berm of the road was not very good. Colin kept saying, "Keep to the middle, dear. Keep more to the left."

Finally, we reached our hotel and carried in our suitcases which were still spilling out rice. The next morning I looked out the window and nearly died. We were sitting on top of a mountain. Now I understood my groom's nagging instructions. I looked at him in disbelief and asked, "Did I drive up that road?"

We visited Lookout Mountain where my Grandfather McGinnis had fought during the Civil War. And on the way back to Detroit we stopped in Homer so Colin could see the town where I grew up.

Married Life

That first evening back we put away our few clean clothes and went to bed for we both had to go to work the next day, I to a new position at the Detroit Public Library and Colin to his job as CPA with Mr. Livermore.

Our second night we put away our wedding gifts and moved furniture until the wee hours. Our floors were bare, but we didn't notice the clatter we were making. The next morning our landlady let us know that we had kept the family awake and would be asked to leave if we continued to make so much noise.

We had been invited to a picnic supper with Lowene and Joe, the man she was dating, that evening. It was late when we returned to the duplex, so we took off our shoes and crept up the stairs. The next morning the landlady came to see us again. It seemed we'd been so quiet she thought we'd moved out.

Father Macdonald and his second wife Ferne had given us money for a wedding present. He'd suggested we invest in something durable like silverware, but we decided carpeting for those bare floors would be more appropriate right then.

Money Matters

As newlyweds, we were paying for furniture and a car and needed to use our money wisely. So, being the careful accountant that he was, Colin set up a budget. Which led to our first spat.

The first time he tried to reconcile our expenditures, I found I had not kept as precise a record as he would have liked. Since I'd been independent for so long, I didn't really realize how important a part of the budgeting process this was.

As Colin got down to the final nickels and dimes, the tension mounted. When, after accounting for my lunches, I couldn't account for the rest, I finally yelled, "I don't know, maybe I bought gum."

At that point Colin decided a budget item for miscellaneous expenditures might be a good idea.

Because of the budget I began to plan meals by the week. On Saturdays I would buy a big roast or a ham and hope I could have it two nights as a hot meal and then as sandwiches and finally use it as stew with lots of vegetables or as ham and scalloped potatoes.

On the first Sunday of my planned meals I fixed a beef roast surrounded by potatoes and carrots and onions and served an extra vegetable because Colin had told me he loved vegetables. With hot dogs for one night and cold cuts for two others, I hoped to make it to the next Saturday.

As the meal progressed I sat there watching the man I loved take slice after slice of meat until there wasn't enough left to make sandwiches. I think he ate one little potato and one small carrot and onion and didn't touch the other vegetable.

I finally said, "Colin that roast was supposed to last us for four days but there isn't even enough to make two sandwiches. My budget is shot."

He looked sheepish and said, "Honey, I've never had such good meat cooked that way. I just couldn't stop. I promise I'll eat the vegetables for the rest of the three days and you can have the meat." I felt so mean that I used the meat and part of the vegetables in a stew on Monday.

That Sunday menu was a very common meal in our home. I realized that by raising our own produce and livestock we probably ate better than many people. Still, I wondered after Colin's extreme reaction to such a basic meal, what kind of a cook his mother had been.

Our First Christmas

Marriage taught us a lot. We found ourselves compromising and learning to share. We'd decided that we would not buy each other Christmas gifts that first year, but send small boxes of Stover's candy to our immediate relatives. Then, on Christmas Eve Colin came in with a beautifully wrapped Christmas present.

To help discipline myself, I'd begun turning my paycheck over to Colin the accountant, who doled out my lunch money and joined me on Saturday's to shop for groceries. Thus, I had no money to buy him a present.

Looking at the gift he'd just carried in, all I could think of was how selfish I'd been. If I'd saved some of my lunch money, I could have gotten him something too. I promptly burst into tears. Colin tried to explain but I couldn't stop crying.

Finally he calmed me down and was able to explain that the gift was for the two of us. He'd saved coupons from the gasoline he bought and had earned enough to get a waffled iron. He loved waffles and I made them often after that.

We didn't have much money for entertainment but we did manage to have a couple of dinner parties during our first year together. For the first one, our guests were three of Colin's fraternity brothers and their wives. Since I was working, I planned a simple meal of ham, scalloped potatoes, green bean casserole and a pineapple-cream cheese salad with ice cream and cookies for dessert.

Unfortunately, one wife was a snob whose wealthy family had bought and furnished the couple's house. She looked at our few pieces of furniture, then checked out our simple cotton curtains and turned up her nose. When I went to serve dinner, she informed me that she was on a strict diet and couldn't have a single thing I had fixed. Then she announced that she was going to starve if she didn't get something to eat.

She finally ate pineapple slices and a roll and asked for milk, which fortunately I had. Everyone else complemented me on the meal. After we ate we played cards and she was a poor sport about that as well. When the couple left, Colin said, "That marriage is heading for the rocks." Sure enough, a year later they were divorced.

Our World Begins to Change

By the end of November 1941, much to our delight, I discovered I was pregnant. One Sunday Colin's brother Dave dropped in unexpectedly on his way back to his home in Washington, DC after a trip to visit Father Macdonald. Food was not my cup of tea right then, so as our meal cooked in the oven, I went out for a walk. Later, after we finished eating, we turned on the radio and listened to music as we visited.

When an announcer interrupted with the news that Pearl Harbor had been bombed, we sat stunned for a very long time. Dave left immediately to return to Washington. Shortly after that he enlisted in the Navy, although at six foot six and a half inches, he had to scrunch down when he took his physical. Because he was a lawyer he was assigned to the Pentagon.

Although Colin received a fairly high draft number, he thought he'd have a better chance of being placed within his field if he enlisted. He chose the Army Air Corp, but was unable to pass the physical because of a recent knee injury. The doctor suggested Colin wait for the knee to heal and then reapply.

Shortly after the first of the year, I began to feel ill. My doctor in Detroit, who thought I was simply upset by the war, refused to examine me. So I went home to consult a more caring physician.

Dad confirmed, as I'd suspected, that I'd lost our baby.

At Dad's insistence, I remained in Homer for two weeks to recover. One night during my extended visit Dad came in whistling with a big smile on his face. When Mom asked him why he was happy, he replied, "Tonight I saved the life of a baby doomed to die of pneumonia simply by giving it a new drug I received this week."

Pharmaceutical representatives had learned that Dad was always willing to discuss new medicines and procedures with them when they called on him. He often invited them to lunch simply to learn all he could about their newest discoveries. One taste of Mom's cooking and they all made sure they timed their visits for mealtime. As a result of one such visit Dad had been selected to test the miracle drug Sulfa that had saved his tiny patient's life.

Both Colin's former landlady and my sister Lowene made sure Colin didn't starve. Still, knowing he would be reapplying for war duty made me impatient to return to our little duplex.

A Clear Case of Abuse

Our landlords, Bob and Betty, had a young son named Bobby. One Saturday not long after I returned from Homer, they had to be gone and had hired a baby sitter. It was freezing outside when Bobby knocked on my door. He was wearing only a thin shirt and no coat and was shivering, so I brought him inside.

He told me the baby sitter was entertaining her boy friend and had locked him out of the house. After I wrapped him in a blanket and fed him hot soup, he climbed up in my lap and asked, "Do you love me, Frances?"

Of course I said yes. I knew with both parents working for the war effort he'd not been getting much attention. I assured him his mommy and daddy also loved him but were working so hard they couldn't be with him as much as they wanted. Eventually, he crawled onto my davenport and went to sleep.

A good two hours after she'd stuck him outside, I heard the sitter calling for Bobby. I decided the irresponsible girl deserved a good scare and didn't answer, so she assumed no one was home. Soon after that, a frantic Betty knocked on my door. I showed her her sleeping son and explained what had transpired, including Bobby's question to me.

Of course the sitter was dealt with and Betty told me later that the extra hugs and kisses she and her husband were now giving Bobby had made him a much happier little boy.

Dr. D.E. and Mrs. Barnett, at Love and Gifford Upjohn's
summer home in Gull Lake, MI, mid 1930s

Frances Barnett
in beaver coat, college years

Frances Barnett at a library job,
college years

Frances Barnett and Colin Macdonald
at Ostego Lake, MI, Sept. 1940

Frances and Colin Macdonald,
Maid of Honor Lowene Barnett,
r. Dr. D.E. Barnett

left and below:
The views Frances saw the
morning after she drove to
their honeymoon stop

Edward Macdonald and his first-born,
Colin, in Michigan, c. 1913-1915

Colin Campbell Macdonald,
5 months old, December 1911

Colin Macdonald and
"Tay-Tay" at 3-1/2

Ruth Woodward Macdonald,
Colin Macdonald's mother,
taken about 1925-1926

Colin Campbell Macdonald,
8th grade, c. 1925

Jean Macdonald,
Colin's sister (1912-2011)

David Grant Macdonald,
Colin's 2nd-youngest brother,
(1913-1986)

Daniel Venn Macdonald,
Colin's youngest brother
(1919-1962)

THIRTEEN

LIFE DURING THE EARLY YEARS OF THE WAR

Colin's knee finally healed and he was accepted by the Army Air Corp and scheduled to go to Officer Training School (OTS) in Florida on September 2, 1942. We stored our furniture and sold our car so he would have money for uniforms and traveling expenses and then off he went to Miami Beach.

I lived with Lowene and kept working until the end of the month, when I was to go home to Dad and Mom. I was pregnant again and seeing an obstetrician at Ford Hospital. The doctor thought he recognized the fancy stitching on the incision from my previous surgery and was pleased when I confirmed Dr. Gatch as the surgeon.

Later, as I walked in to his office for my last check-up, I heard him say to his previous patient, "Now Mandy, you've had five babies and you're going to have this one without me." When he saw me he said, "I'm in the Army now and I won't be here to help you." Then he shook his head and added, "I don't know what they want with a baby doctor. Just wait, I'll be looking down a bunch of G.I.'s throats."

I was to remember his prophecy a few years later.

We All Learn to Ration

We were at war and it didn't take long for people to realize what that meant. Long working hours for both men and women at aircraft plants, ship yards, and steel and metal and other war material factories. And because so many items were funneled into the war effort, things became hard to find and everyone was issued ration coupon books.

Even with proper coupons, food (especially meat and coffee and sugar) and gasoline and construction materials were scarce. Metal was so precious to the war effort that drives were held to pick up scrap metal of any kind. Eventually, even the foil from gum wrappers was being recycled.

City dwellers had an especially hard time. But it didn't take long for them to find a plot of ground and plant vegetables.

Mom and Dad and I were better off than most because we had meat from the farms. In addition, our grocer offered to exchange coffee and sugar with us for pieces of meat. Like everyone else, we were especially careful with our gasoline coupons and made every visit to the farm and elsewhere count.

Dad was happy to have me home. All the younger doctors had been called up, so his practice had almost doubled. Once more I drove him to see his patients, kept his books, and helped Mom clean the office. All that activity helped keep my mind off the separation from Colin.

Together Again

While Colin was in OTS, I waited and waited for my first dependent's check. When I asked Colin why it hadn't come, he said that one of the civilian secretaries kept refusing to forward his papers. She insisted no one named Macdonald spelled their name with a small d. I suggested that it was time to visit his C.O.

As it turned out, my naive husband didn't realize the secretary was making a play for him, using the delay to insure he would have to keep returning to her desk. It seemed this had happened before. She paid dearly for her foolishness when the C.O. sacked her. I then received my six months back pay pronto.

When Colin's basic training ended, the rumor was that they would be shipping out soon. He begged me to come to Florida so we could spend his last few weeks together. I could see how exhausted Dad was becoming from the stress of his expanded practice. But he agreed that I should be with Colin.

Colin found a temporary room for me in a hotel on Miami Beach. It had blackout curtains and twenty-five watt bulbs with the ocean side of the bulbs painted black. No lights were allowed after dark except in a windowless room such as a bathroom.

One night there was a hurricane scare and all officers with wives were allowed to be with them. Fortunately the storm skirted our area and there was little damage; however wreckage from a German U-boat washed up on shore.

The next day things were much calmer and Colin decided to go swimming. I remained on the patio, sharing a table with a family I had met. There were several people on the beach, but no one was venturing into the water.

Colin had just gotten in the ocean when an officer came up to me and said, "There's a shark out there. Tell your husband to leave the water." I rushed to the shore and called and waved and Colin got out in a hurry.

Protective Measures

The beach was patrolled constantly. During the daytime you were not really aware of this, but at night no one was allowed to go onto the beach. German bodies from the submarine had begun washing ashore. (Which probably explained the presence of sharks.)

One night I woke up to hear a voice calling out, "Halt, who goes there. Advance and be recognized."

When no one answered, I heard, "Corporal of the Guards! Corporal of the Guards!" and a new voice demanded, "Who goes there? Answer or I'll shoot." This time a feeble voice whined, "Can't a man walk his dog?"

"Not on the beach after dark," the corporal responded. "If I'd had anyone but a greenhorn recruit on duty tonight, you'd have been a dead man. Now, get off this beach."

I was shaking as I listened by my window, but also glad of the drastic measures the service was taking to insure our safety.

A Place to Live

Rather than the accounting assignment Colin had wanted, after OTS he was sent to code and cipher school at Morrison Field in West Palm Beach. Evaluations had noted his instant recall and flare for detail and the Army Air Corp felt those skills would be best utilized in code work.

With so many men in training, there were few places to live and most of the better apartments were filled. We began looking the moment we arrived in West Palm Beach. The only place we'd found had so little security that Colin was afraid to let me live there alone, so we checked into a hotel for the night.

We'd just gone to sleep when a train whistle woke us. It sounded as if the thing was right beneath us. Engines chugged and whistles blew all night. The next morning we discovered the hotel was over a roundhouse where engines were switched.

Later that day we found a furnished efficiency with a Murphy bed (a bed that pulls down from the wall), an alcove with stove and refrigerator, a closet and a small bath with shower. A second door opened onto a court surrounded by three other buildings of apartments. It was quiet and comfortable.

The office, with the only private phone in the building, was across the hall from our apartment. Just outside the office door was a pay phone.

One afternoon I walked the beach, picking up shells after a storm had blown in, which proved to be a mistake. Colin rushed me to a doctor who gave me couple of pills and put me to bed with my feet elevated to prevent me from losing a second baby.

Colin pulled down the bed and I crawled in, getting up only for bathroom privileges and to eat.

I soon discovered how thin the walls between apartments were. Our neighbor, a young soldier from Tennessee who'd recently married a much older woman, came home unexpectedly one afternoon to find her in bed with another man. Since I was a captive in my own bed I learned a few new expressions. The shouting was so fierce that the personnel in the office got a good language lesson too and promptly evicted the couple.

Shortly after that, we discovered that a great many women were hanging around military bases and marrying soldiers simply to get monthly checks. Some, using different names and addresses, married more than one man at a time.

A Startling Experience

It was while I was living in West Palm Beach that I had my first encounter with a frightening phenomena that was to reoccur several times during the war years and then sporadically during other stressful periods in my life.

One Saturday Colin was asked to fly to another city with a group of buddies to a football game. I thought he needed a break from caring for me, so I encouraged him to go. That evening, as I was sleeping, or perhaps only dozing, I suddenly visualized one of his friends calling for help to block the opening where a window had blown out of their plane. The image of someone stuffing a pillow into the gap was very vivid.

When Colin returned I asked him about the pillow. His mouth fell open and he said, "It was a parachute, not a pillow, but who told you? " We were both baffled by the episode but could find no explanation.

A Second Episode of ESP

When Colin finished his code and cipher course, he was sent to a base at Homestead, Florida. There was no housing in the area, so I made plans to return to Homer on a train that was scheduled to leave in two days.

The night I bought my ticket, I couldn't sleep. Every time I closed my eyes, I kept hearing my father's voice calling out my nickname, "Bill William. Bill William." I sat up in bed and looked at the clock. It was about five A.M., but still dark outside.

The phenomena continued inside my head as I went into the courtyard and began walking. Suddenly the voice stopped calling me. At that precise moment somewhere in one of the trees, a bird began singing the most beautiful song I'd ever heard.

With a heavy heart, I returned to my room. Somehow I understood that, although I would always be the country doctor's youngest daughter, my father's life was over.

Reality Returns

I couldn't go back to sleep, so I paced the courtyard off and on most of the morning. I wanted to call Mom, but I didn't have any change to feed the pay phone and the apartment building's office wasn't open. All I could do was wait.

About ten that sunny morning of November 18, 1942 a very somber Colin came home. Before he could say anything, I hugged him and asked, "What time did Dad die?" He stood there dumbfounded, then asked how I knew. I told him, "It happened again," and related my experience.

I learned that they'd tried to call me very early that morning but, since no one was in the office to answer, had phoned Colin at Homestead. By all accounts, my sixty-five year old father had died at the precise moment the voice I'd been hearing fell silent.

Because any time Colin took off would be deducted from the days we were saving for our baby's birth. I chose to take the train alone. I knew I'd need Colin even more after the birth because Mother did not drive. Some of Dad's mourners seemed shocked that Colin was not by my side, but we were a practical couple and based our decision on what was right for our future.

Dad had treated the needs of the residents of Homer and its surrounding communities with skill and compassion for over thirty years. His patients responded to his devotion by overflowing the church at his funeral, which was held in the Baptist Church because the Christian Church we'd attended had burned down.

When Mother tried to buy a burial plot in Rushville's East Hill Cemetery, she discovered Dad had already purchased crypts in their newer mausoleum, the construction of which had been placed on hold until the end of the war. Also reserved were crypts for Doc's family and Colin and myself if we chose to use them. Thus Dad was temporarily interred in the cemetery's much older mausoleum and later moved to the newer building.

Closing a Link With the Past

After Dad's death, it was left to Mother and me to settle his estate. We children turned over our share in the farms to Mother for her lifetime. Then we sold his pharmacy and office furniture to another country doctor and locked the office building itself. The hardest task was collecting the outstanding accounts on his books. The vast majority of Dad's patients were honest people, but a few refused to pay what they owed.

Dad had known his heart was failing. But, despite often admonishing his critically ill patients to put their own affairs in order, he did not have a will. This classic case of the doctor telling patients to "do as I say, not as I do" and Mother's failure to make provisions for her own death would return many years later to haunt those they left behind.

A Much Delayed Arrival

Our baby was due the first of March in 1943. But March first came and went and still nothing happened. I kept writing Colin not to take his accumulated leave until I went to the hospital and promised Mom would call him if that day ever came.

After two-and-a-half weeks had gone by, my doctor in Shelbyville suggested that I move into town where he could keep better tabs on me. Thus I spent almost another two weeks in the Be-Bo Inn next to the hospital until my reluctant child decided the time was right to enter the world.

(Amazingly, the Be-Bo Inn, which later became the Hunter Hotel and then a private home, is still standing. Its newest reincarnation - *Note: as of the 1999 date this was written* - is as a restaurant, The Hamilton House.)

Finally, early Sunday morning April 4, 1943, after an especially uncomfortable night, Mom decided the contractions I'd been having had gone on long enough and insisted I go to the hospital. I had intended to walk, but the landlady insisted on driving me those few yards.

Of course, as soon as I registered, the contractions stopped. But they soon started again and around seven o'clock that evening my daughter was born. She weighed six pounds, four ounces and I was told she was one of the longest babies they'd ever delivered.

The doctor held her in his arms and said, "Look at your Mommy." When she raised her head off his arm, he said, "You're too young to do that." Then he laughed and added, "Well, I guess you *are* a month old aren't you?"

As promised, Mother notified Colin that mother and daughter were both fine. He made plans to arrive in Indiana in time to drive all of us back to Homer after my mandated ten day hospital stay. Unlike today's *drive-by* deliveries, women were encouraged to remain until both they and their child were stronger and the minor surgery often performed to aid in delivery had begun to heal.

When I'd gotten my first glimpse of the baby, she had a red face and, because of her unusually long length, was very skinny. The fingers of her little hands were like claws. I was still a bit woozy from the medication I'd been given and told my nurse, Mary Meloy, "She's not very pretty is she?"

Mary said, "She's beautiful. She has a nice round head and the sweetest face. You've just never seen any new born babies."

The next day when I was no longer drugged, I looked her over and realized Mary was right. She *was* a beautiful baby. Still, I worried because they'd told me that when she'd been delivered, the umbilical cord had been wrapped around her upper arms, allowing her to move only the lower portions of her arms. As it turned out, she had no problems other than an aversion to having her arms pinned to her side by unsuspecting playmates.

All the private rooms were taken, so I spent my first night in the maternity ward. After the delivery of another baby, while the mother was still in recovery, Mary brought the newest infant by my bed on her way to the nursery. Despite being born slightly early, the baby was very fat and very wrinkled. Mary held her up and whispered, "Now this is an ugly baby."

When a private room became available they moved me into it. The nurses had all known and loved Dad and took very good care of me, but how I wished he could have been there.

Love At First Sight

After Colin drove us home, he looked at his daughter and held her tenderly. He even changed her diapers, which was not a common thing for men to do in those days. Colin loved her so much. The name he chose for our child was Patricia. He didn't like a combination of long and short names like Patricia Ann or Patricia Sue and thought Patricia Macdonald was long enough for any child, so she has no middle name.

(I should point out that, although she was called Pat or Patty for much of her early life, my daughter is now known as Trish. To avoid confusion, that is how I'll refer to her throughout the rest of the book.)

I didn't have enough milk to nurse, so we had to put Trish on a bottle. Colin fed and burped her like an old pro, but she soon began projectile vomiting, eagerly drinking an entire bottle only to lose the same volume in moments. My doctor was ill, so Mary Meloy recommended a pediatrician in Indianapolis. He diagnosed an intolerance to manufactured formula and prescribed a mixture of barley water and Carnation Milk.

Creating barley water was an involved procedure and I swore he chose that solution because he thought I looked like a nervous mother and needed to be kept busy. Nevertheless, Trish loved it and it loved her. To this day she likes barley in things like vegetable soup.

When Colin returned to Homestead, he learned that his C.O. was looking for someone to straighten out their financial system. Jumping at a chance to return to the work he loved, Colin volunteered and was appointed acting Budget and Fiscal Officer. Unfortunately his new position did not relieve him of his regular duty. Instead, he was expected to work on the financial books late into the night and rarely got enough sleep.

The Pain of Goodbye

I kept Colin posted on Trish's development through daily letters. At one month she rolled from her back to her tummy and then back again. Later I put her on the bed with a big pillow in front of her. I had just turned to reach for a little shirt when down went the pillow and Trish rolled down on top of it. She sat up alone at three months and at four months started scooting. Then she learned to crawl — but only in reverse gear.

Because he'd been doing double duty and had never really liked working with codes anyway, in mid August of 1943, Colin filed for permanent transfer to the finance department. Nineteen days later, he learned that his request had been too late. He was being shipped out and would have a twelve day leave near the end of September to put his affairs in order.

Except for his travel time, he spent all of those precious twelve days in Homer. The entire time he was there he was extremely tired and suffered from what he thought was a severe cold. As a result, he wouldn't kiss either the baby or me on the mouth. In photos taken during that visit, Colin is kneeling, awkwardly holding Trish away from his body to avoid spreading his cold, rather than cuddling her close as he would have preferred.

I kept thinking that if Dad had still been alive, he would have known what to do to make Colin well.

Trish was now four months old. Colin watched her crawl backward and circle around to get to her toys. He decided this wouldn't do, so long-legged Colin got down on the floor to teach his daughter the right way to crawl. Trish just sat and watched his demonstration, then laughed. Finally, he tried moving her arms and legs in the proper motions, still without success.

The days slipped by so fast. He would look at Trish and say, "Honey, she's ours, all ours, your's and mine." When the day came for me to drive him to the Indianapolis airport, he went to the car and came back three times to pick her up and hug her. Finally with tears in his eyes he handed her to Mother and came out to the car where I was waiting.

As we embraced he said, "Since I can read my coded orders, I know I'm not being sent into battle."

And then we left.

When I returned much later, Mom told me that she'd run out to report that Trish had begun to crawl forward, but we were already driving away.

FOURTEEN

BORROWED TIME

When Colin had originally arrived at Homestead, the camp was still under construction and had far too many men for its only completed barrack. Cots were crammed tightly against each other, foot lockers stowed beneath them. To get into bed each evening, it was necessary to crawl over the foot of the cot.

The arrangement put each man's head only inches from the other's. The boy next to Colin had a terrible cough, so Colin suggested that everyone alternate sleeping positions - one man's head at the top of the cot, the next's at the foot. This solution put each man's head five or six feet apart and relieved them from such close approximation to each other's germs.

Finally, after much urging from Colin and the others he was keeping awake, the boy went to the camp doctor. That night when the men returned, the barrack was being fumigated. The boy had been diagnosed with TB and sent home.

Because he was exhausted from working day and night, when Colin began displaying flu-like symptoms several months later, he failed to connect his own illness to that of his former bunkmate. But the damage had already been done. Exhaustion had weakened Colin's immune system, leaving his body little defense against such an invasive disease.

During his layover in Miami Beach on his way to his new assignment, Colin walked around the camp getting further orders and proper clothes for his new post. Finally, he felt so bad he decided to visit the camp doctor to get something for his cold.

When he explained he needed something before he shipped out, the doctor laughed and said, "Oh, you've just got buck fever." (A phrase used to describe the fear many young men felt when faced with going into combat.) Colin said, "No, I can read my orders. I know where I'm going and it's not into battle."

Even after that, the Doctor refused to take his temperature or give him any medication. He just continued to laugh.

Colin's destination was British Guiana, South America (now known as simply Guyana), which had not yet become a combat zone. He was flown there in an unheated plane. Other soldiers piled blankets on him because he was chilling so much. Since he had to wait to see the doctor after landing, Colin walked around in the hot sun. He also mailed me an army newspaper to let me know he'd reached his destination. Soon after that he collapsed with 105° fever and was rushed to the hospital.

At first, the doctor accused him of having every kind of venereal disease, but finally decided to take an X-ray. The diagnosis was swift. TB had rapidly spread through his lungs during the plane ride and his walk in the hot sun.

Finding a Way Home

I received the newspaper letting me know Colin had arrived safely, but nothing more for several weeks. The doctor in British Guiana tried to get Colin transferred back to the U.S. for better treatment, but couldn't get him on a plane because every available aircraft was assigned to ferry severely battle-wounded soldiers to stateside hospitals. In the meantime, Colin asked a grey lady (a hospital volunteer) to write a note for him.

After a short time Colin asked if the doctor would let him try to get himself on a plane. The doctor said, "What the hell do you think you can do? If you're so smart, go ahead and try."

That afternoon (November 9, 1943) the doctor walked in to find Colin packing, dressed and waiting to be released and transported to his plane. Later, Colin told me that doctor's astonished look was something to see. The doctor said, "How did you do it? I've got two very sick boys I'm trying to send home for better care." Colin gave him a code word, but told him not to abuse it and to use it right away before it was changed.

Left in Limbo

I wasn't notified when Colin returned to the States. For several months I still believed he was in British Guiana. Since I'd received no further correspondence from him via the grey lady, I knew nothing of his condition. In truth, he'd been transferred to a regional hospital in Coral Gables, Florida for evaluation.

It was during this period that I first began having what was to become a reoccurring dream. I was always on a train. I knew Colin was close but I couldn't see him or find him. There were three men with me on the train but I could never see their faces. One was very tall. The other two were much shorter. They would speak to me and then I would cry and the dream would end.

The dream made no sense but it was very disturbing.

Finally another grey lady wrote to tell me Colin was on his way from Coral Gables to Fitzsimmons Hospital in Denver. She suggested I try to connect with his train when it came through Chicago, but provided no clue as to when that might be. With no way to know and space on most trains reserved for military personnel, I had no choice but to wait until someone let me know when Colin actually reached Denver.

Unfortunately, before I received such notification, I smashed my thumb quite badly in the car door. A few days after that, a man selling Persian rugs came to the house. When I refused to make a purchase, he became very angry and slammed the storm door on my thumb, bruising it from yet another angle.

A few days later my hand and arm began to swell. I spent the night before my appointment with a doctor walking the floor with the pain. When morning came, red streaks were radiating up my arm and I realized I'd developed blood poisoning. By the time the ordeal was over, I'd lost the end of my thumb, leaving the bone exposed.

A good dose of antibiotic would have prevented such a thing, but most of the medicines we now take for granted were developed during or after the war. Sulpha powder was the doctor's only weapon, but the infection had progressed too quickly for it to do more than halt further damage.

The doctor, afraid I might contract TB of the bone, refused to let me travel to Denver until the wound completely healed. I could not have gone in that condition anyway, since I couldn't use my hand to pull up my girdle or dress myself.

A Frustrating Wait

Since I couldn't go to Colin, I resigned myself to keeping him informed about our daughter's progress.

Trish was an active little girl. Once while Colin was still in British Guiana, Mother put Trish in her high chair to feed her. I came into the kitchen just as Mother yelled. Trish was hanging by one foot, face down. I grabbed her and put her back in the chair.

By the time she was six months old she would crawl to a chair, pull herself up, and walk around it. If I got close to her she would take one step to me.

Arbuckle's Grocery had just gotten some candy bars, the first they'd received since the war had begun. We raised our own meat and grew our produce, so we had unused coupons for those items. I used some of them to buy two bars of Hershey chocolate.

When I came in, I tossed one bar to mother, then opened my own and broke off a piece. Trish was sitting on the floor. She pushed up to her feet, ran to me, grabbed the bar and took a bite. I sat there and watched her devour the rest of that candy, too amazed at her walking to take it away. From then on she ran, rather than walked, everywhere.

The Brown girls next door liked to put Trish in her buggy and walk her around the square. I had to strap her in because she stood up all the way. If only one of the girls took her out, she had to push with one hand and hold onto Trish with the other.

I kept Colin's uniformed picture on the top of our upright piano. I'd take it down, show Trish the ribbons saying, "This is your daddy." Soon she'd point to the ribbons and say "Da Da."

After she learned to walk she started climbing and I caught her standing on the piano's sheet music support. She was holding on to the top of the piano with one hand and reaching for the picture with the other, saying, "Daddy, Daddy."

When she was about nine months old, Wallace Inlow, a family friend, brought his wife to visit. Wally was in his Navy uniform. After inspecting this stranger for a while, Trish climbed into his lap to play with the ribbons on his uniform.

She was jabbering away in her usual baby talk when, suddenly she looked at her daddy's picture, then back down at the ribbons. Then she grinned at Wally and said, "Daddy."

Wally held her close and said, "No, darling, but I wish I were." The couple had no children. When he turned to look at me, tears were rolling down his face.

Time to Go

My thumb was almost healed and I was anxious to see Colin but several things stood in the way. I knew no one in Denver. How would I find an apartment that would take children? And where would I find a sitter I could trust? I couldn't ask Mom to come with me. She had the house and gardens and the farms to look after. Leaving Trish in Homer was not an option either. Although she did her best, Mother was no match for a lively toddler over an extended period.

Finally, Love and Gif offered to keep Trish while I went out to see Colin and look for a place for my daughter and myself to stay. In the meantime, Father Macdonald decided to go to Denver in my place. A fellow lawyer whose wife had been cured of TB had suggested Colin's father learn all he could about his son's condition and write the head of the U.S. Health Service to see if Colin would be better off in a private hospital.

Because neither the Health Service nor the Army would pay for private care, Colin's father decided we had no choice but to leave Colin where he was. On his way back from Denver, Father Macdonald stopped in Homer. (I think to chide me for being a neglectful wife.)

By now, Trish was about fourteen months old and a very busy little girl. I needed to help Mother with dinner, but Trish's delight in a new game she'd devised - rolling cans of baby food (commercially jarred food was not available yet) under our feet - was causing a problem.

I finally picked her up, walked to the sitting room, plunked her down on her very proper grandfather's lap and said, "If you can entertain her for just five minutes, I'll get dinner on the table." He laughed and Trish looked up at him and laughed too. After that, they got along fine.

Colin's father enjoyed mother's good cooking and ate heartily. (Later, every time I visited him he talked about that dinner. I don't know why the Macdonald men were so impressed by simple home cooking.)

Once Trish was in bed, we talked about Colin's case. Father Macdonald had called in a specialist who was not very encouraging. I think he'd thought I'd been procrastinating about my thumb until he saw it and I explained how hard it had been to care for Trish and to dress myself without Mother's help.

Before we retired we walked outdoors. Colin's father looked up at the stars and listened to the crickets and a big bull frog down at the creek. The next morning, he said, "I had a hard time falling asleep here. I can't ever remember such quiet." Peaceful little Homer was vastly different from noisy Detroit.

A Painful Separation

I'd explained to Father Macdonald that Love and Gifford considered keeping Trish for awhile as their contribution to the war effort since they had no one in the service.

At least my sister and her family would have little trouble communicating with my daughter. Shortly after her grandfather's visit, Trish began talking in sentences, such as, "Mommy, see the titty tat? See Mommy? Now go bye-bye. I want the dolly."

On my way to Love's I stopped at Lowene's so she could see Trish. While I was there, Father Macdonald brought his wife Ferne to call. We were all visiting when Trish took Lowene's hand and announced, "Go to kitchen, get cookies," then led her there and pointed at the cookie jar.

I think Father was amazed at the change in her because he asked, "Did she say what I think she said?" I nodded. Lowene put some cookies on a plate and while she finished the refreshments, let Trish pass them to the rest of us. When Lowene brought in the tray with ice tea, she laughed and said, "Not quite the way I'd planned to serve, but with such good help, how could I refuse?"

I spent a few days with Love and Gif in Kalamazoo for Trish to get acquainted with the family. Gif had bought a bottomless playpen, thinking he could keep her safe from the water when they spent time at their lake cottage. He set it up and put her in it. Trish sat on the grass staring at the playpen. Then she got up, walked to the side and lifted it up and walked out.

Gif said, "I think I just wasted my money."

It was so hard to say goodbye to Trish. I took the train to Chicago and cried all the way there.

Denver

Before I was allowed to see Colin, I had to don a gown and a mask. I was shocked by how gaunt he looked. As soon as he saw me, he began crying. He'd waited so long to see my face and now there I was hidden behind the mask.

I bent to kiss him through the material and he turned his head. It seemed to me the elaborate precautions were unnecessary if we weren't in danger of exchanging germs. Eventually, after several more visits, I abandoned both the gown and mask.

We talked until it became obvious he was tiring, then I went back to the Officer's Club to unpack. The next morning I began my apartment hunt. Everywhere I went, I was told no children were allowed. It soon became clear that I'd have to take a single room until I could find a place that would accept Trish. In the meantime, I needed something to fill my idle hours and steer my thoughts away from Colin's ill health.

Father Macdonald's friend and his wife had met my train and we'd kept in touch. One day the man called to ask if I'd be willing to volunteer at the Denver TB Association office. The morning hours they assigned me proved to be just what I needed.

Every afternoon I visited Colin and stayed until visiting hours were over that night. I sometimes fixed him a snack and often brought food to tempt his appetite because he was so thin.

He didn't get much sleep because he was on the lower floor of a wooden barrack. Men nearing release were above him and played cards until the wee hours, moving chairs and tables across the wooden floor. On top of that, he'd been forced to endure the unsuccessful process of having first one lung and then the other collapsed in an effort to trigger the healing process.

A Remembered Conversation

Gif had asked me to look up a sorority friend of his sister's while I was in Denver. The woman invited me to church with her and then return to her home for dinner. Due to the shortage of meat they maintained a rabbit warren, so that's what we ate.

The next day I went to work but began to feel ill and returned to the room I'd rented in the home of a couple named Moreau. When I did not appear for dinner, that evening, Mrs. Moreau came to check on me. I was feeling much worse, so she took my temperature, which was 105°. Since this was as high as the thermometer registered, she became very worried.

After an unproductive call to a doctor and the nightmare of finding a taxi in their suburb of Aurora that would cross into the territory of its rival Denver cab company, my landlords got me to Fitzsimmons, where I was promptly admitted. They then visited Colin and explained my absence.

Because I'd eaten rabbit, the emergency room doctor suspected I might have tularaemia (a serious disease contracted by eating wild rabbit that has not been cooked long enough.) But once I said the family had raised them, he relaxed and began treating my fever with sulfa. At one point I suffered such severe chills that my bed began banging against the wall and they had to pile hot water bottles and blankets around me until I warmed up.

The next morning, I recognized the new doctor who came to see me as my obstetrician from Ford Hospital in Detroit. Before I could say anything, he said, "Open up and let me look down your throat." Remembering his last comment to me before I left to join Colin in Florida, I started laughing.

"Do I know you?" he asked.

"That's the last thing you said to me at Ford Hospital," I told him, "'Just wait, I'll be looking down a bunch of GI's throats.'"

By then he'd begun to check my abdomen. He took one look at my scar, recognized the distinctive stitches, and said, "Dr. Gatch's patient. What did you have?"

"A little girl," I replied.

After my exam, I was kept on the sulfa, and given a test which showed that I was suffering a strep throat that had settled in my kidneys. Eventually, the medicine did its job and I soon felt well enough to return to my work at the TB Association.

Making Changes

Colin's doctor seemed to have a sadistic streak, or at least a very poor bedside manner. One day I went into Colin's room and found him crying. He said, "I'm not going to get well." It seemed he had asked his doctor a question and gotten a very ugly reply. So Colin had said, "You don't care whether any of us live or die do you?"

The doctor said, "Hell, no," and then walked out.

I knew I had to do something or Colin would completely lose his will to live. I spent that night contemplating what to do. The next morning, I went to the grey lady who had written me when Colin first arrived at the hospital. She was the widow of the former head of the hospital and suggested I go to the C.O. and try to get Colin transferred.

As I waited outside the CO's office, I thought about how to explain my request. I knew bringing up professional ethics and criticizing Colin's doctor would be a bad idea. The food was cold when it reached Colin's room and the barracks were noisy so I decided that would be my approach to the situation.

What I didn't know was that the grey lady had already told the C.O. about the doctor's remarks. When I got in to see him, he told me only that he would consider my request. That following afternoon when I went to see Colin he wasn't in his room. When I asked a nurse if Colin was in therapy, she snapped, "No, he was moved to the main building." On my way there I met the doctor, who gave me a strange look but didn't speak.

When I finally found Colin, he was in a lovely room and delighted to be there. He also liked his new doctor. He said, "My doctor came in while I was eating, grinned and pointed to the bread and said, 'that's edible, you know,' so I ate every bite."

A Welcome Break

Except when I was ill, I was with Colin every spare moment. I had gotten into the habit of stopping at a little restaurant when I left Fitzsimmons to eat a late supper. One night it was crowded and a woman I had seen in there several times asked me to sit at her table. Thus I met Nat and her husband Alden who was a orderly at Fitzsimmons.

One Sunday Nat asked me to go with them and a very young orderly on a drive around the area. The boy was very homesick and told me I reminded him of his mother. I was about thirty-four at the time, but stress had made me look — and feel -- much older. The outing gave me my first close look at the Rockies, but I found the drive up the mountains rather scary.

Keeping in Touch

Love was wonderful about writing us letters to let us know how Trish was adjusting. At first she'd refused to eat or to talk after I'd left and would only nod her head in response to their questions. Because of my problem with my thumb, I hadn't completely weaned her from her bottle, which had upset Love and Gif at the time. Now, they were thankful that she still accepted her nap time and bedtime bottles.

Eventually, Trish adjusted to her new surroundings and began to thrive. I was happy about that, but equally sad. Colin and I were missing hearing all her cute sayings and watching her grow. Still, I was grateful Love wrote as often as she did to fill us in on what was happening and to reassure us that having a little one around again was still a joy.

Nancy, Love's youngest, was about eleven, so my sister was a bit removed from the days of dealing with a toddler. Trish's adventures on a single morning was all it took to remind her.

Love's bridge club was coming for lunch. Her live-in cook and housekeeper, Pearl, was busy getting things ready so Love was on her own with her active charge while arranging a centerpiece of flowers for the table. She went to the kitchen to dispose of some excess greenery, only to return to the sight of Trish in the middle of the table, pulling out her carefully placed flowers and chanting, "Pretty, pretty."

Love carried Trish into the living room, hoping to keep her out of trouble. There Trish pulled every book off the bottom shelf of the bookcase. Of course she also thought it was just as much fun trying to cram them all back in any way she could.

Just when Love thought she had things in hand once more, she was called back to the kitchen. In preparation for the bridge club, she'd set up four tables and placed two decks of cards on each one. This time when she returned, she found all eight decks mixed together on the floor.

At that point, Trish was quickly fed and put down for a nap. When the guests came they found my normally poised and in charge sister on the floor in the middle of the living room, separating cards. Love's letter assured us that her friends found the situation hilarious.

During the war there was a lot of talk about conserving gasoline and not driving unless it was necessary. Love wrote that she saved all her errands for Saturday when Gif was there to help her. Apparently the importance of such conservation had made an impression on Trish. One day she and Gif remained in the car while Love took in some dry cleaning. Trish looked at Gif and asked, "Uncle Gizzard, is this trip necessary?"

Gif and Love also took eight millimeter movies of Trish and sent Colin a copy. I rented a projector to show the film on the white wall of his room. Soon after that, Mother Macdonald came to see Colin, so I rented it again.

Below: Frances and Colin Macdonald, December 1940

Right: Colin and Frances Macdonald, Alpha Xi Delta Dinner Dance, Hotel Olds, Lansing, MI, February 14, 1941

Frances and Colin Macdonald, West Palm Beach, FL, October 1942

Colin Macdonald, West Palm Beach, FL, October 1942

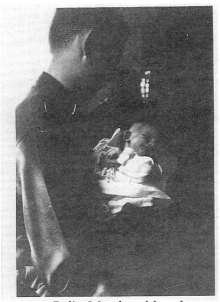

Colin Macdonald and
daughter Patricia,
age 1 week

Frances Macdonald and
daughter Patricia,
c. 1943

Colin and Frances Macdonald,
with daughter Patricia, his
second and last visit,
September 1943

Colin Macdonald,
last time he held daugher
Patricia

FIFTEEN

INTERPRETING THE NIGHTMARE

Eventually, when Love tearfully wrote that they were getting so attached to Trish that they were afraid they wouldn't be able to give her up, I knew I had imposed enough and should go and get her. Colin, who said he was feeling better, agreed. I began to make arrangements to go home.

Penicillin had been discovered and was proving successful in some TB patients. The Upjohn Company had been manufacturing it for some time but couldn't keep up with the demand. They had opened a new facility and were about to up their production, so Gifford added a note to Love's letter suggesting I ask the C.O. if the drug would help Colin.

When I asked, I was told that because it had only been proved effective on TB of the bone, they felt they could not justify using such a precious commodity to experiment on lung patients. The C.O. then asked, "What makes you think you could get a supply for him anyway?"

I explained that I didn't know if I could. He then said, "Even if you could, we wouldn't use it on him." Of course I went out crying. Just then, I saw a bunch of German POWs coming down the hospital staircase. They were looking around the lobby and murmuring, "Wunderbar, wunderbar."

All my anger spilled over. I was so mad that because of their old war my husband was so sick. Naturally about then I ran into the obstetrician from Ford Hospital who wanted to know what was wrong. I said, "They refuse to try penicillin on Colin," and he let me cry on his shoulder until I could compose myself.

A Painful Transition

When I left Colin to return to Kalamazoo to retrieve our daughter, our parting was especially painful. Colin knew I would not be returning any time soon. Because housing was so tight, I'd never been able to find an apartment what would accept a child.

Love had put out a picture of me and kept telling Trish that I was her Mommy. But Trish had begun to refer to Love as Mommy because Nancy did. Even so, when they met me at the train and asked her who I was, she said, "That's my mommy."

I spent several days at my sister's so Trish could get used to me again. While I was there, Gifford asked if I'd told the C.O. at Fitzsimmons exactly where I'd proposed to obtain penicillin. When I assured him I hadn't, he revealed that even before I reached Kalamazoo, he'd had a request from Fitzsimmons for extra penicillin. We decided my former obstetrician had told the C.O. about our connection after comforting me that last day.

When we finally left for Mother's, everyone wept. Pearl, the housekeeper, was on her knees in tears. I know how traumatic it must have been for Trish to be torn from them and to switch homes once again as well.

While I was gone, Mother had sold the house in Homer and bought one at 58 W. Hendricks Street in Shelbyville so she would be nearer to Doc. Because she was having the house remodeled, we rented rooms from a woman named Lucy Hiatt.

Also renting rooms from Lucy were two school teachers, Jane Durrenberger and Jesse Bodem. Our first night there, Trish had a hard time settling down. After all she'd been through, she suddenly found herself sleeping in a strange bed with a mommy she hardly knew. I put her down and when I thought she was asleep went down to the sitting room to be with the other adults.

When she came looking for me only moments later, I knew I'd have to stay with her. I tucked her back in and assured her I'd join her as soon as I washed up. While I was in the bathroom she went looking for me again. At that point, one of those straight-laced teachers said something that frightened her and by the time she found me she was almost hysterical. I promptly gathered her in my arms and forgot about my bath. When Mother's house was finally ready, I was quite happy to leave.

The Nightmare Continues

The upsetting dream I'd been having since Colin had been in British Guiana had returned to plague me while I was living with the Moreaus in Aurora. I had hoped it might go away when Trish and I were together again. Instead, I discovered it had accompanied me to Shelbyville. I often woke up frightened by the nightmare of being alone with three strange men on a train.

While I was home I wrote Colin everyday. Trish would scribble a letter too. I listened carefully to what she was telling her daddy and then wrote it in my letter to him. This kept her busy for a few minutes. She played with her toys and with Doc's two children, Chuck and, Dan who was just walking and not very steady on his feet often stumbling into toys. I read lots of books to all three, usually when Mother wanted to nap.

When the grey ladies at Fitzsimmons wrote me that Colin was going down hill, I knew I needed to return to Denver. But the problem of finding a place where Trish could be with me remained. As a diversion one evening I attended a high school basketball game. The Red Cross contacted Doc, and after the game he handed me a telegram from the doctors that said Colin was gravely ill and they thought I should return immediately.

The Red Cross got me on a Burlington train that was leaving for Chicago the next morning. Doc and Hanne agreed to help Mother take care of Trish. I called Father Macdonald and learned he was already making plans to go to Denver. Colin's mother was ill and could not travel.

By now, the dream had plagued me several nights in a row. That night it returned, more vivid than ever and lasting much longer. I was on that train and Colin was near but I could never find him. The three men were always present but I could never see their faces. One was very tall, the other two much shorter.

When I got to Chicago, Burlington did not show a reservation for me on the connecting train to Denver. After begging them to find a space, I remembered the telegram in my purse. That was all it took. I later learned my Denver reservation had been made with the Sante Fe line in another terminal.

The Porter made up my berth and promised to call me early for breakfast. After having the dream yet again and being awakened by some rough track, I finally fell into a restless sleep. I awoke to find it was nine o'clock.

I asked the porter why he had not called me and was told we'd been delayed by a wreck and I still had time to eat.

The dining car was empty, but after I ordered, two gentlemen asked if they could join me. One asked if I'd slept well. I told them the first half had seemed a little smoother than the last and I thought it might be because they were trying to make up time. I found it difficult to keep up a conversation, so I apologized, explaining why I was on the train.

To my surprise they said, "Yes, we know. The train reserves one berth for such emergencies." One said, "I'm the public relations representative with the Burlington line," and the other added, "I'm his counterpart with the Santa Fe. We had to transfer to my line after the wreck."

After breakfast one of the gentlemen took my bill. I said, "Oh no, no stranger pays my bill." Then they laughed and the man from Burlington said, "We had a bet on as to which railroad bed was the smoothest. Sante Fe lost."

The Sante Fe man said, "I like your idea that maybe the haste in trying to make up lost time made it less smooth." When they left, they both gave me their best wishes that everything would be well with Colin.

Father Macdonald's friends again met my train, but the time table kept changing, due in part because we had to sit on the sidings to let troop trains, which had priority, go by. It seemed as if everything was conspiring to keep me from Colin's side.

A Final Moment

When I finally reached the hospital, Colin could hardly breathe. He'd developed pneumonia in both lungs. I had just told him, "You've overcome other hard times and you're going to beat this too," when his father arrived.

On his heels was a Chaplain who'd not been to see Colin in all the time he'd been ill. When he entered, he immediately began, "Ye, though I walk through the shadow of death . . ."

Colin looked up at me and whispered, "Oh, no." Then he closed his eyes and gave up, falling into a coma. Pushing me aside, the Chaplain continued his prayer. Less than an hour later, on Jan 6 1946, Colin was gone.

Living the Nightmare

My return ticket allowed me to accompany Colin's body to Indiana. Father Macdonald was able to purchase a ticket as well. When we reached the train and got on, the same Burlington P.R. man was there and asked me if all was well. I burst into tears and said, "No, I lost him."

He leaned over and put his arm around me and said "I'm so sorry." Colin's father was quite upset about this until I related my experience at that breakfast in answer to his demand of, "Who is this man?"

Just then the head of the Denver TB Association office where I had worked all those months came over and greeted me. He also put his arms around me when I explained about losing Colin. Father Macdonald's face was a study. I think he was wondering what kind of a daughter-in-law I was. I quickly introduced them and they soon found they had several acquaintances in common.

I said my goodnights but when I crawled into my berth, I couldn't sleep. Suddenly, I thought of my dream.

Colin was in the baggage car with two privates guarding him, so of course I couldn't see him. The tall man in my dream was Father Macdonald. The P.R. man and the head of the TB office were the two shorter men.

I cried all night and looked awful the next day.

Closing a Painful Chapter

The funeral was held in the Wyatt Funeral home in Rushville. Colin's casket was closed because he'd lost so much weight. Very few people attending really knew this sensitive, caring and lonely man I'd married. Those who came did so in respect for my family.

Colin was interred beside my father in the old mausoleum. An honor guard gave a military gun salute and presented me with the flag that had covered his coffin.

And then it was over.

SIXTEEN

LIFE AS A SINGLE PARENT

The Government took care of everything associated with Colin's death but the funeral home expenses. His father offered to pay Wyatt's and, not knowing what my financial situation was going to be, I accepted his offer. He was amazed at the less than hundred dollar charge, most of that for the transportation from the train to the mortuary and then to the mausoleum.

We returned to Shelbyville and a meal furnished by friends and women from the Christian Church. Soon after, Colin's father and his brother Dave left, as did the rest of my family. I was struck by the realization that I was now alone with a child and partially responsible for Mother's care. The idea was formidable.

There was lots of red tape to get Colin's estate settled and letters and consultations with the Veterans Division to determine what I would have to live on. Most of my income would consist of Social Security's small survivor benefits and Colin's Veteran's pension. But, with his precise and practical nature, Colin had set up his G.I. insurance so that there would be no lump settlement, but a monthly income that continues to this day.

I considered moving to a college town and getting a library job. But then I thought about the expense of an apartment and baby sitters and food and health care. After adding in my remaining debt to my siblings and weighing the total against the meager funds coming in, I felt I would be better off staying with Mother, at least until Trish was in school.

Thus I settled down to quiet widowhood.

Tough Questions

Trish still remembered writing letters to Colin and one night she asked, "Why don't you write Daddy?"

Since she was not quite three, one of Doc's teacher friends had taken care of her during the funeral. I realized that, with my personal grief and confusion of dealing with the overwhelming problems of becoming a widow, I had never taken the time to truly explain what death meant.

Now, I tried to tell her that her Daddy had gone to Heaven, but at three, such concepts were impossible to understand. She grew angry and stamped her foot and said, "I don't want my Daddy to be in Heaven. I want him to come home and play with me like other Daddies do."

When I explained that could never happen, she wept most of the night. Every so often I would hear those sad little hiccups. Mommy didn't sleep that night either.

After that she launched a concentrated effort to find a Daddy. She often rode her trike in front of the house. A sweet old gentleman (old enough to be my father) who passed by on his way to work in a men's clothing store would always run his finger up one of Trish's blond curls and greet her by saying, "How do you do?"

While we lay in bed one night, Trish asked why I didn't find her a father. I told her it would have to be a very nice man to take her Daddy's place. She thought awhile and then announced, "I know a nice man -- the Mr. How Do You Do man."

I explained that he already had a wife and was too old to be responsible for a child. Then, knowing my daughter, I made a point of bringing her inside to play during the time I knew he would be going to and from work.

A few nights later the subject of daddies came up again. Trish said, "I know another nice man."

When I asked who the man was, she replied, "Why, Uncle Gizzard." I explained he was married to my sister, her Auntie Love. She thought for a long time about the problem and then said, "Couldn't we just *borrow* him?"

I made the mistake of telling Love about the conversation. She in turn told Gifford. From then on, whenever Love and Gif came to visit Mother, Gifford would ask, "Frances, do you want to borrow anything?" I, of course, reacted by turning brick red.

Eventually, I began to emerge from the grief that had seemed all consuming and joined a young couple's group at the Christian Church. At one of our monthly pitch-in suppers I left Trish playing with other children while I helped in the kitchen. When I returned, I found her on the knee of Mr. Lesley Day.

As Trish ran off to play again, Mr. Day watched her a moment and then, with tears rolling down his cheeks, confided, "She asked me if I would be her daddy."

Trish Goes to School

The fall after Trish turned three, I sent her to private nursery school. A few weeks later the teacher called and said, "I need to put her up with the older group. Is that okay?" Thus, she was only four when she entered kindergarten. Then, because she didn't meet the local school system's birth date requirements, her kindergarten teacher had to revise her curriculum so Trish wouldn't be bored repeating the class as a five-year-old.

Mixed Signals

Trish kept saying she wanted a red wagon, so I put one in lay-away for her April birthday. Then, whenever she asked for a wagon, I made up some excuse as to why she couldn't have one. Once I said, "They're expensive. I don't know if I can afford one."

Of course Trish shared this remark with her teacher. I was paying tuition for nursery school, so the teacher called my sister-in-law Hanne to ask about my financial situation. Hanne laughed and explained about the pending birthday surprise.

A Lesson Well Learned

When she was about four, Trish ran away to play with a couple of girls who lived on the other side of Tompkins Street, which ran beside Mother's house. Tompkins had become a race track for teen drivers coming from the high school several blocks away and was very dangerous.

Before I went after my wayward child, I broke off a little switch. Remembering the sting of my father's peach tree branch, I gave her only one little tap before I explained why she didn't cross the street. Then all the way home I would touch the switch on the ground behind her and repeat, "It's too dangerous to cross that street without Mommy watching you."

Shortly after that incident, Dave and Doris Macdonald brought their daughters Jill, a year older, and Joan, a year younger than Trish, for a short visit. Dave was watching the girls bounce a ball on the sidewalk in front of our house.

When the ball bounced into the center of the street and then stopped, he was amazed to see Trish holding back both his girls and warning them not to run into the street. Very soberly she informed them, "Mommy says she can get a new ball. But she can't get a new me if I run into the street and get hurt."

Choosing a Grade School

Unfortunately, the wagon incident was not the end of the poverty discussion. Trish had heard her uncle discussing the plight of students who attended Major School in the poorer part of town. Doc felt at the time that the children were being short changed because the best teachers were rarely assigned to Major and many parents worked long hours and were unable to help their children as much as was needed to offset the problem.

With typical misunderstanding, Trish informed her kindergarten teacher that because we were so poor, she would have to go to that "poor Major School". As it turned out, we lived on the dividing line between two districts and had a choice of either Major or Colescott Schools. I chose Colescott because for Trish to reach Major she would have had to cross a state highway, a busy city street, and a very dangerous railroad.

Playing Games

Trish's usual playmates were her cousins, Chuck and Dan. One thing they especially enjoyed was playing hospital. She had a lot of blocks which they used to outline rooms in a hospital. Long flat blocks became beds. Ones in unusual shapes would create a fancy entrance to the imaginary building. A toy ambulance with a siren brought patients to the hospital.

Many times this game lasted for over an hour. At some point Dan, who was the youngest, would stumble and scatter the blocks which usually ended the game. Of course, the boys always wanted to run the ambulance. All three children could make that siren ring through the house. Eventually life imitated play when both boys became doctors.

Once when Trish was about four, Mother had a headache. I wanted to keep Trish quietly occupied so Mother could rest, so we lined up chairs in a single row in the living room and played train. Trish was the conductor and then the engineer.

I made up names of places where we were going. Trish would say, "All aboard!" and I would go to a seat. She collected the ticket and then she sat on the front chair. She had just called out Kalamazoo when the door bell rang.

A Mrs. Chambers had dropped by to visit Mother. When I returned from waking her, I found the very proper Mrs. Chambers had joined in the play. She was handing her ticket to Trish, who was delighted to have another passenger.

As Trish grew older her favorite game became cops and robbers. Her cousins and various neighbor children and even visiting relatives were enlisted as players. Once a game began in the afternoon, paused for dinner and then resumed until we adults called everyone home because of darkness.

A Special Friendship

Mother had chosen to live only a block from Shelbyville's downtown area, so she could walk to the grocery store, the bank and church. Because most families preferred to be closer to their children's school, Trish had few children her age to play with.

The parsonage of the Second Baptist Church, which served a black congregation, was located in the middle of our block. Rev. and Mrs. Noel Hord's children thus became Trish's primary playmates. Freddie and Gloria were a few years older; Kathy was around the same age; and baby Noel was the typical tag-a-long little brother. Later, son Kenny completed the family.

The children visited back and forth. We had a little table and chairs that I would put in our fenced-in back yard for their many tea parties. The Hord children were the sweetest and nicest behaved children she played with. When it snowed the children pulled each other on their sleds and made snowmen and angels in the back yards. Sometimes I took a turn pulling the sled as well. They had so much fun, they never wanted to come in to warm up.

One summer Freddie constructed a miniature golf course in the parsonage's back yard, using tin cans for the holes. As the oldest, he took responsibility for the others and kept them busy by staging relay races and other sports events in the alley behind the houses. When Trish and the Hord children were together, the neighborhood always rang with laughter.

Like Mother, Like Daughter

Once Freddie asked Trish to go with Gloria and Kathy and him to Gloria's music teacher's home near the city park. Although

Freddie told her she couldn't go unless her mommy said it was okay, Trish couldn't find me right away. (I was in the basement, doing laundry.) Afraid that the others would leave her, Trish told Freddie a fib and said I'd given my permission.

While Gloria had her lesson, Freddie took the two younger girls to the park. I thought Trish was playing at the Hord's, but when I went down to get her I discovered she wasn't there.

Rev. Hord, who did carpentry work to supplement his ministerial salary, came home for something just then and assured me that Trish was probably with his children. Then he offered to go get her. As he brought her back in his truck, he talked to her about telling the truth and explained how worried I was. After that, even as a teenager many years later, she never left home without telling me where she was going and asking permission.

Looking back on the incident now, I realize how brave Rev. Hord was that day. Although race relations in our schools were very good for the times, our town was not without bigots and the Ku Klux Klan was very active in some parts of Indiana. For a black man to be seen with a white child in his vehicle could have been disastrous. Nevertheless, Rev. Hord did not hesitate to respond to a mother's panic about her missing child.

Changing With the Times

Although Shelbyville continued to maintain a separate school for black children attending grades one through eight, our high school had been integrated since the 1920s. Then, a year or two before Trish began first grade, the school board realized the system had reached another crossroads.

As one of the oldest school facilities in town, the Booker T. Washington building had begun to deteriorate. At the same time, there were so few black students that some grades contained only one or two children. The City Council decided it would be less expensive to integrate the rest of the school system than to make the extensive repairs needed.

There was much careful preparation involved in making sure both black and white students adjusted to the integrated classes. Teachers received special training and then talked to the P.T.A. groups of each school involved. When the transfer students attended orientation at each of the three previously all-white schools, their mothers came with them.

Thus, while no one would deny there were some minor problems, Shelbyville spared itself the terrible public conflicts that erupted decades later in so much of the country.

When Trish started off for her first day at Colescott, Gloria Hord held one hand and Freddie Hord held the other. Freddie told me, "Don't worry, Mrs. Macdonald, I'll take good care of her." And I knew he would.

Beside being well behaved, the Hord children were excellent students. Although the family moved to a church in Terre Haute, Indiana when Trish was nine, I later learned that Freddie completed high school at fifteen and then graduated from college.

Still later, after a busy career that brought him great personal satisfaction and many public awards, Rev. Hord and his wife Jessie returned to Shelbyville. Trish and I visited them and learned that Fred (as he now prefers) had earned his Ph.D. and was a college professor. Gloria or Kathy (I can't remember which) followed in her mother's footsteps and became a librarian; the other teaches; and little tag-a-long Noel is a businessman whose success earned him a write up in a major national magazine.

A Different Kind of Prejudice

When Trish was seven, my sister Love offered to pay our tuition at a month-long parent and child summer institute being held at Vassar College in Poughkeepsie, New York. The institute courses focused on child development techniques designed to teach single parents how to deal with problems unique to children in one-parent homes. Courses were also offered for parents raising children in difficult circumstances.

After we registered I took Trish to her dormitory. Children stayed in one dorm; parents, in another. This allowed the staff to evaluate each child in a variety of situations. A fixed period each day and most of the weekend hours were set aside for joint parent and child activities. While their children enjoyed camp-like diversions, parents attended classes in child psychology, participated in group discussions and attended cultural events.

By either coincidence or design, Trish and her roommate Jill Maddox shared a birthday - April 4, 1943. The ratio of counselors to children attendees was four to one. Trish and Jill and two little boys were assigned to a male counselor, Pete Berg, a Ph.D. candidate whose participation was part of his thesis preparation. His mother was on staff as the nurse for my dorm.

Next morning at breakfast Jill's mother and I were paged and told to go to our children's dorm. We found Jill crying. I assumed she was having problems being separated from her mother and they needed privacy, so I took Trish out on campus.

Before I could ask if she knew why Jill was upset, Trish suddenly asked, "Mommy, what's a Jewess?" I thought for a minute and finally said, "It means she has a different religion. Do you remember when Bobby Siebert brought his scrolls to school and talked about them and his religion?"

She nodded and then said, "Jill said I wouldn't like her when I found out she was a Jewess. She cried all night and I don't understand why."

This one was a little tougher to explain to a child her age. I finally said, "Sometimes, awful, mean people say they don't like the Jews and treat them very badly." She didn't say anything, so after a moment, I asked, "Do you like Jill?"

"Oh yes, she's nice and she can play the violin."

"Well then, you tell Jill you love her just because she's Jill and she's nice and that you don't hate Jews or anyone else."

Later, I had lunch with Jill's and Pete's mothers. Jill's mother was so pleased that Trish had told Jill that she loved her and asked what I'd said to her. When I repeated our conversation,

Pete's mother protested that I'd sugar-coated my explanation and that there was much more to the problem than that.

I agreed, but argued that what I'd said was sufficient for an unprejudiced child of seven and added that Trish's best friends were the children of a black minister.

By this time we had the attention of everyone at our table and most of the dining room. Someone wanted to know how others in our town felt about Trish's playmates, so I explained how Shelbyville had dealt with the integration issue. I also pointed out that my brother taught high school and coached basketball and that he had three black players as well as two Jews and an Italian on the team and everyone got along just fine.

Activities at the Institute

The children had lessons in music and crafts and swimming and nature, as well as hiking or biking to places of interest. In the evening they gathered in the dorm's sitting room where Pete played guitar and taught them folk songs. Everyone loved his silly versions of "Billy Boy," which included Billy's lady love wearing her wedding gown up-side-down.

I had my own schedule, taking courses in crafts and personal appearance and radio and speech. But my most important classes were the lectures by the Director, Mrs. Langmuir, which helped us understand what parenting was about.

Mrs. Langmuir, illustrated her points with stories. She shared the experience of a couple who'd been taking her course. Their little boy had been given permission to stay up a short time for his parents' adult party and allowed to greet their guests.

Apparently the boy had been learning his anatomy. Much to the horror of his parents he asked each of the first guests if they had a penis. They quickly distracted him, apologized to their guests, and hurriedly called Mrs. Langimuir to ask what they should do. "Instruct your guests to simply answer 'yes' or 'no' and that you'll explain later," she told them.

After interrogating a third couple, the child turned to his parents and announced that those who wear pants have penises and those in skirts don't. He then went off to bed having sorted out, for the moment, the difference between men and women. Of course, times have changed a bit since then. Clothing no longer makes the man or woman, at least in that regard.

Mrs. Langimuir also taught us that all caring parents, married and single alike, worry that they're not doing a good job. Then she provided us with skills every parent needs to raise happy, productive children. Among these are:

- Tackle big problems rather than nitpick little things - an unmade bed is less important than consistently ignored homework. (As we say today: Don't sweat the small stuff.)

- Realize how big a parent seems when they tower over a child - sit or kneel down to the child's level.

- Quietly spoken instructions capture a child's attention much quicker than shouted commands.

- Allow some control over basic routine by offering choices. (For example, instead of saying, "Make your bed right now!" I learned to say, "Trish, sometime before breakfast, please make your bed." This gave her a choice - she might make it right away or she might play for a moment. But when she heard my call that breakfast was almost ready, the bed did get made, sometimes better than others.

- Provide opportunities for a child to explain thoughts and ideas. For example: Ask what he thinks about the way a storybook character handled a particular dilemma. *Then listen to his response without arguing.* If his views seem a hundred and eighty degrees from yours, gently point out other options he might consider in similar situation.

Giving a child options to make up their own mind helps them grow and become more independent. Of course, when it comes to safety issues and dangerous behavior, quick and firm responses always take precedence.

A Mother and Child Experience

Every weekday morning Trish and I had an hour together when we could do anything we wished. She would show me her craft work and I would listen to her tell about her activities like feeding the nature center's pet raccoon and learning to play the triangle in music class. I also learned that during a nature hike they'd discovered the remains of an old shack and were now recycling the materials to build a tree house.

One thing Trish wanted more than anything was to learn to ride a bike. We had purchased one before we left for Vassar, but she hadn't gotten beyond the training wheels stage. When her group had gone bike riding that week, Trish had been forced to ride a big tricycle, which she hated.

I'd mastered a Model T as a child, but never ridden a bike and had no idea how to teach what I didn't know. That Sunday we went to the campus quadrangle where I attempted to help her.

As long as I held on she could ride. But when I let go, she lost her balance. A man whose son was also there learning to ride suggested I put one pedal up for her to push down to get her momentum. Using this technique, I held the back of the seat until she'd steadied herself. Then she pushed off without looking back. Not realizing she was on her own, she yelled, "Let go, Mommy!"

When she turned the corner and could see I was still standing at the exact spot where she'd started, the most beautiful smile lit up her face. It was a wonderful moment.

Swimming at the Institute

Because the Institute believed that little boys and girls' curiosity about each other's bodies was a natural thing, children under the ages of ten were allowed (with parents' permission) to swim *au naturel*. Trish and Doc's two boys had gotten beyond that

170

curiosity stage long ago, so I voiced no objection when she wanted to take off her suit before taking the test that would allow her to swim in the deeper part of the large indoor pool.

After failing her first try because she couldn't see where she was going, she tried again with her eyes open wide. This time she passed and was soon jumping into the sixteen foot end where Pete was already working with the others from her group.

By the end of the Institute, she'd become a real water baby. This proved to be a blessing, because Shelbyville's public pool was only a few blocks from Mother's house. During the summer the pool offered a wonderful diversion for Trish. It also kept her out of mischief when I eventually found work.

Frances Volunteers

While at Vassar, we were exposed to many cultural activities. We once attended an address by Eleanor Roosevelt and also traveled to New York City to see South Pacific on Broadway. But the bulk of our time was devoted to our various classes.

One requirement of our Institute speech class was that we prepare and give a talk before the rest of the class. Unlike Mom, I hadn't received lessons in elocution and had never spoken before a group. When our teacher asked for a volunteer to give the initial speech, my first instinct was to hide. But I realized it would only get harder if I procrastinated, so I raised my right hand, forcing it up with my left before I could change my mind.

I decided to make my speech amusing, hoping my stories would temper my lack of skills. I practiced for several days and once I felt I was ready, delivered my address on why I'd come to Vassar.

First I mentioned that my sister had paid my tuition and for that to happen, I knew my parenting had to be in deep trouble. Then I admitted that I'd needed help in dealing with a three-generation home. I also talked about the fun of having to snatch my child off the street every day before she pigeonholed any man who came along and asked them to marry her mommy.

171

The stories earned laugher and when the teacher asked for criticism, there was none. She commented that my speech was well organized and then asked, "Did anyone else notice that when she volunteered, she forced her right hand up with her left?"

And I thought I'd been so casual about it.

A Revealing Report

At the end of the Institute, everyone was given a psychological profile of their child. Trish's said they first believed I'd made her shy and quiet and that she didn't participate with the other children and had no initiative. That is, until they began to look beyond their first impression.

Trish had been the one to instigate the "pinch club," which, if I remember correctly, you could only join if someone in the club had pinched your bottom. The idea for the tree house had also originated with Trish, who was then perfectly satisfied to serve as architect and crew foreman while her playmates did the bulk of the actual construction.

As they observed her more closely they saw that she was the organizer of many of the things the group did. The teachers' final conclusion was that she was a very intelligent and well-balanced little girl with good leadership skills.

Going Back Home

After our seminar, we spent a few days in New York City, visiting Rockefeller Center and Radio City Music Hall, where the highlight of the tour was seeing Trish appear as if by magic on the newest electronic invention to sweep the country - a TV set.

We also took a boat ride around Manhattan and went to Central Park. For a child who'd spent most of her life in rural environs, New York was a fascinating place. I was pretty impressed as well. Our only mistake was climbing the stairs of the Statue of Liberty early in our stay. From that point on, our calves were so tender we had to help each other up and down the curbs.

SEVENTEEN

OUR LIVES ON WEST HENDRICKS STREET

Shortly after our trip to Vassar, Colin's youngest brother Dan and his wife Ruth and baby daughter Kathy came for a visit. While they were there, my brother-in-law shared some of his experiences as a career Air Force pilot.

During World War II Dan led a bomber squadron, flying sorties out of Egypt. He had many frightening experiences, but his closest call came on the way back from a successful night raid.

Dangerously low on gas when he returned to home base, he discovered it was under attack. Not knowing whether he'd be able to take off again, he had to set the plane down on nearly invisible terrain in an uncharted part of the desert.

Next morning they got the all clear signal and inspected the landing spot. High dunes rose on both sides, but directly ahead lay the only clear stretch of sand as far as they could see. He was able to take off and return to base with only a little spare gas.

After the war Dan was assigned to Strategic Air Command. Again his description of a particular flight kept us enthralled.

While ferrying an aircraft to the States from a base near the Bering Straits, Dan was radioed that a bomb had been hidden on board. He and his crew had only minutes to abandon the plane in the skies over British Columbia.

Dan set the auto pilot to take the plane away from land, then everyone bailed out with Dan going last. Moments after he jumped, the plane exploded.

Most of the men landed almost waist high in a bog, but one young boy came down in a tree and broke his leg. Once everyone was accounted for and a litter had been fashioned for the injured man, they started struggling through the muck. The navigator had grabbed his charts but the day was overcast. Finding reference points in the desolate territory proved to be difficult.

Eventually heavy ground fog forced them to stop. They could hear search planes overhead, but had no flares and knew they were hidden by the fog. The next day dawned clear but, unknown to them, weather around the nearest bases had worsened. Once planes were back in the air they mistakenly centered on the area where bits of the plane had come down.

As the days wore on, the men became cold and wet and discouraged. Dan, who like Dave and their father was several inches over six feet, had weighed two hundred pounds when they took off. When he and his crew were finally rescued over a week later, he weighed a hundred and twenty-five.

We were visiting Doc's the evening Dan told his stories. Nine-year-old Chuck, who'd recently seen Hollywood's version of a war picture, asked Dan if everyone had shouted "Geronimo" when they jumped. Dan said, "No, we just wanted to leave as fast as we could and were more concerned about getting out alive."

That visit was the only time Trish saw her Uncle Dan. He died years later from what I believe was a form of leukemia while still a relatively young man. I was living in Indianapolis at the time and once again had been warned by an episode of ESP.

Ruth later remarried and Dan's three children took their step-father's name.

Trish's Adventures

I gave Trish ballet and tap lessons and she was in several programs. She looked very pretty in her frilly costumes, but in

174

truth, she was a tom-boy who preferred playing baseball and the other things that were considered strictly male pursuits at the time.

We had a movie theater around one corner of the block we lived on and she loved the B westerns and any picture about World War II. I think perhaps that was where she dreamed up some of her more dangerous adventures, many of which I probably never found out about.

I do know Mother once caught her preparing to jump from the roof of our neighbor's bathroom to our bathroom roof across the picket fence - a distance of over eight feet. I dread to think of the disastrous results if she'd succeeded.

Another time Trish and the Hord children spent the day playing in the coal bin at the end of the dead-end alley beside Wickizer's Tippecanoe Press building. I think her greatest delight when they all emerged into the sun was discovering that she and her friends now shared the same skin tones.

Even though she was a tomboy, Trish loved to play with dolls. She had a Jerry Lee doll that was her favorite, as well as a Terry Lee doll. Most of her allowance was spent on doll clothes and comic books. Often I came outside to find neighbor children reading comics from the toy box we kept on the back porch.

Mother's House on Hendricks Street

While I didn't pay Mother rent, I did keep the car Love and Gifford had given her in good condition and helped with groceries. One year I added a screened back porch to the house, where Mother liked to sit after dark in the cool of the evening.

The house itself consisted of a living room and a small parlor where we kept the piano and where the kids often played on rainy days. A dining room, kitchen, two bedrooms and a bath completed our living space. The basement where we canned food and washed clothing had a cement floor which Trish found was an excellent place to roller skate during the winter.

Huge maples that shaded the porch and small yard where Trish organized baseball and croquet games lined our side street.

Driving Mother

Indiana's summer nights could be hot and muggy. Since we had no air conditioning, we often took long rides in the country to cool off. Sometimes I'd ask one of Trish's friends to go along.

Road signs were few so I sometimes made a wrong turn or got a bit lost. Once we ended up in someone's barn yard and had to ask for directions. The kids got a big kick out of that. Later I heard Trish ask a friend, "Would you like to go driving with my Mommy and me and get lost?"

History Repeats Itself

When Trish was in third grade, so many baby boomers were enrolled that two rooms held far too many students for one teacher to handle. Several parents whose children were doing well in school were asked to allow their children to skip a half grade and join a class that had only twenty-five students.

I debated about the request for several days, remembering how my father had believed that skipping children into an older peer group pressured them socially and that the younger students often lost out on information they needed.

The teacher emphasized that to keep Trish busy she had to assign her extra reading and was rarely able to give her individual attention. Then she begged me to permit Trish to go on. I still had misgivings, but finally capitulated.

I know now that my father was right (as usual). Trish would have been happier had she remained in her own grade. By skipping she was thrown into a new peer group. While most were sweet girls, one in particular often made Trish feel like an outsider.

A Glimpse of the Future

Trish loved reading and we read a great many books. The library was across the alley from our back yard and she often sat on its steps or leaned against a particular pillar to read, even after dusk. When I wanted her to come home, I'd whistle a special combination of notes based on the number of syllables in Patricia. Often, she was so absorbed in her reading that it took more than one whistle to break through her concentration.

Many years later, when her first book was published, she returned to the library to speak about growing up on that block. Before she left, she had her husband take a photo of her leaning against that same pillar, reading her own work.

A Gathering of the Clan

Dave Macdonald and his wife Dorie's three daughters, Jill, Joan and Julie were fourteen, twelve and five the year Trish turned thirteen. Dave thought the cousins should get to know each other, so he invited Trish and I and Missy, the fourteen-year-old daughter of Colin's sister Jean for a two-week visit at Dave and Dorie's home in Bethesda, Maryland.

Dave, practicing law in Washington, D.C., had just presented a U.S. Supreme Court case. He had a beautiful home with a lovely garden and pool, as well as domestic help.

Missy and Trish and I were eager to tour the nation's capitol. Jill and Joan had seen the sights and would have preferred spending their days in the pool, but agreed to come along. (I'm sure Dave laid down the law about being good little hostesses.)

We'd driven to D.C., so I became chauffeur for our little tours. The current subway system was years away, but parking in the Capitol was much easier than today, so we were able to park within walking distance of most destinations. Still, driving proved to be a challenge. Once I accidently turned the wrong way onto a one-way street and suddenly found myself facing oncoming traffic while trapped in a car with four screaming teenagers.

A disaster was averted by the quick actions of an understanding policeman who provided an escort to a cross street and directions to where I was trying to go. I'm still not sure which upset the girls most - my driving mistake or their own embarrassment at being with such a crazy adult.

In the 1950s no one wore shorts into businesses or public buildings and even slacks were frowned on for women, so the girls were all wearing the long, heavy cotton skirts and net petticoats that were in fashion. Washington was sweltering and they complained constantly.

One day they took off their shoes and socks and walked barefoot along a low wall in front of the Library of Congress building. I received a lot of disgusted glances from local residents and tourists alike for permitting such a thing.

Testing What I'd Learned

Some time after Trish and I had attended Vassar Institute, I was asked to speak about the experience at a Lion's Club luncheon. Even though I'd mastered the skills of delivering a speech, I was still scared to death.

I began by saying, "In my speech class at Vassar I was told to take a deep breath, remind myself that no one in the audience wanted to be in my place, and then relax. I've done all that. But I wasn't prepared to look out and see fifty pairs of *male* eyes."

When the place erupted in laughter, I relaxed and continued, emphasizing Mrs. Langmuir's teachings about raising children. I also stressed that parents should be in control, but before correcting a child they should let their anger cool and first give the child time to explain their side of the situation.

I found that once you made one speech, you were in demand for every other organization in town. By the time I'd talked before the various service clubs and school PTAs and at meetings of Girl Scout leaders, I felt like a veteran.

The Perfect Position

Later that same year, Rev Ford, minister of the First Christian (Disciples of Christ) Church, called on Mother. She'd transferred her membership from Homer but I hadn't.

I think he had an ulterior motive beyond bringing me into his flock, for he soon asked if I would consider becoming church secretary. After making sure the salary would not exceed the income restrictions the government placed on my pension, I accepted his offer of a part-time position.

The church had never had a paid secretary before, and neither Rev. Ford nor I knew exactly all the duties. My first task was to put out the Sunday bulletin. Our next project was to publish the first-ever printed budget for the membership to see.

After purging our outdated membership roll and requesting sample budgets from other churches our size, we prepared our own budget for the church's board of directors to review.

The chairman was shocked to see in black and white how meager our minister's salary was when compared to other churches of equal size. The records also revealed that, at times, there had not been enough money to buy coal for the furnace and that the minister had used his own savings to warm the church for Sunday services.

The following Sunday a revised budget, doubling the minister's salary, was presented to the congregation and a fund drive was begun to finance needed expenditures. Despite such support, some improvements proved a hard sell with the board.

Our church office was on the second floor over the parlor in which the board held their meetings. The only phone in the building was in the hall at the foot of the stairs. My request for a separate office phone or an extension had been turned down.

One Saturday when I was preparing the church bulletin, Clyde Yater, the board chairman, called a special meeting. That morning the phone rang constantly. In order to get to it before the caller hung up I had to *run* down the stairs. Tiptoeing was an option only on my return trip to the office.

Not realizing anyone would be in the building, I'd worn hard soled high heels to work. I must have raced down that stairway a dozen times that morning, making an awful clatter.

That next week I got an office phone.

Foxy Grandpa's Counterpart

As secretary I also kept track of maintenance needs. One of the pews at the back of the church had a large crack in the center of the seat. It only held three people. But if the two on each side got up faster than the one in the middle, the seat often grabbed the slower churchgoer's clothing or pinched his or her bottom and would not let go until the others were reseated.

I requested that the pew be removed or repaired, but no action was taken. After several more complaints, I discussed the issue with the chairman's wife, who'd once been the pew's victim.

Mrs. Yater said, "If I sit on one end of that pew next Sunday and you take the other, Clyde will have to sit in the middle. Then, when we rise for prayer . . ."

That Sunday when the minister asked us to pray, Mrs. Yater and I jumped up before Clyde could react. He yelped, "Ouch," glared at me, then turned to his wife and said, "You planned that." His sweetly smiling missus said, "Yes, I did."

Monday morning the bench went out for repairs. I'm sure Foxy Grandpa was grinning right along with the board chairman's wife.

Expanded Duties

I worked as the church secretary for over ten years. When Rev. Ford accepted a calling to a larger church, Rev. John Faust took his place. He and his wife Mary Ellen were a wonderful couple and the church membership grew under their direction.

They say a willing worker gets more than their share. This was true in my case, for suddenly the board added the secretaryship of the Sunday school to my duties. I'd already been recording church donations and making the bank deposits for some time, so soon after that I was also made church treasurer and became a board member.

As the church grew, a full time secretary was needed, but I often drove my Mother to see about farm business and Trish

180

already felt neglected when I wasn't there when she came home from school. Thus, Imogene McCain was hired to help me.

After Rev. Faust accepted another pastorate, Rev. James Horner replaced him. Once again, our membership increased. Jim, as he preferred to be called, had a beautiful voice and often sang solo with our choir.

An Addition to the Family

Trish had been very lonely since the Hords had moved. One day while I was working, she came racing in with a motherless black and white kitten cradled in her arms. It was so small its eyes still hadn't opened. It looked like a rat.

She'd never had a pet, but always wanted one and was sure I'd let her keep it. I was just as sure the poor thing wouldn't live. Then I took one look at my daughter's pleading brown eyes.

Our new kitten was awfully cute with her four white feet and lopsided face, one half white with black whiskers the other black with white whiskers. Trish immediately named her Socks. I bought kitty food, but when we got home, I realized the kitten was too little for adult cat food. The doll bottle I tried first didn't work. Finally, I found a medicine dropper and fed her with that.

Because Socks was so tiny, I fed her every four hours. It took a long time to get any nourishment into that little tummy. That evening we made a bed for her in a box in the basement. Trish, who'd promised to take care of the kitten herself, slept like the dead, but all night long I heard this pitiful little mewing through the furnace register.

The next night I wound up an old alarm clock and put in with the kitten and she slept between feedings. Surprisingly, or perhaps not so surprisingly considering all this loving care, Socks survived and grew. Once her eyes opened, I tried a dish of warm milk, hoping she'd learn to lap. Instead, she immersed most of her face, then licked the milk off her fur.

Trish thought this was hysterical. But without a mother cat to show her what to do, Socks was lost. She finally learned to drink by kissing the milk. Her method was quite noisy and very funny to watch, but she never did learn to lap properly. I sometimes think she survived in spite of my care. Eventually, she grew to be a very lovable companion for Trish.

Going Cruisin'

As Trish grew older, she and her friends attended the high school basketball games. They took turns eating at one another's houses before a parent drove them to the gym. The girls liked for me to pick them up after the game because I usually took them to a favorite drive-in for Cokes before driving everyone home.

One evening while they were watching the older teenagers "cruising" the restaurant in their cars and fantasizing about the day they would have their own licenses, a woman named Rose Ann Johnson who was a friend of one of girl's parents pulled in beside us. She was driving a beautiful powder blue convertible.

Trish's friend quickly introduced us and then the girls went into a whispering huddle. Rose Ann was a lovely girl who worked at the telephone company and had never married. She also had a keen instinct about those giggling girls. After we chatted a bit, she gave them all the ride they wanted so badly and had been whispering about.

Rose Ann and I found we liked many of the same things and eventually became good friends. Even though she was much younger than I, our friendship lasted until her death in 1998.

Above: Edward Macdonald and grand-daughter Patricia in Homer after his visit to Colin at Fitzsimons Hospital, Denver, CO, c. 1944

Right: Patricia Macdonald, probably while living with the Upjohns, c. 1944-45

One of the wards at Fitzsimons Hospital in Denver, CO, November 30, 1944

Frances and Patricia Macdonald
c. 1947-48

Patricia Macdonald, c. 1947-48

Dan and Chuck Barnett with Patricia
Macdonald, having a tea party in
Cora Barnett's backyard,
c. 1948-49

Patricia Macdonald,
c. 1948-49

EIGHTEEN

NOTHING LASTS FOREVER

When Trish was a Freshman my ESP reappeared once again, perhaps because I was dealing with the stress of raising a teenager. One evening I was restless and felt that something was wrong. Trish was tired and wanted to go to bed, but I said, "Please sit with me a while. I have a feeling we may get a call."

About fifteen minutes later Dave Macdonald phoned to tell me his mother had died. We talked for a few minutes and by the time we hung up, my restlessness was gone.

Trish made very good grades during her high school years, so I bought a used car for her to drive to school, a red 1954 Chevrolet convertible. That's when my worries really began.

One evening Trish and several other kids piled into her current boyfriend's car and drove to Indianapolis to a movie. The weather changed abruptly and soon a sleeting rain left the roads a sheet of ice, so they took a back road home to avoid traffic.

While I waited anxiously for her to come home, I suddenly visualized a red truck pulling out from a side road, unable to stop. In my vision, the boy who was driving the car Trish was in, slammed on his brakes, did a three hundred and sixty degree donut, and missed the truck by just inches.

When the kids finally arrived, I asked by how much they'd missed the red truck. Their mouths dropped open and one asked how I knew. All I could say was that I had seen it in a vision.

A Devastating Error

While hospitalized in the mid 1950s for a severe bleeding ulcer, Mother was accidently given type O positive blood instead of the O negative she needed. Although the doctor who was called in managed to revive her, her heart had actually stopped before he arrived. Unfortunately, in the interim, her brain had been deprived of oxygen. She was never quite the same.

Fearing stress from managing the farms had caused her ulcer, an outside manager was hired. But when she relinquished that responsibility she seemed to go downhill much more quickly.

Hardening of the arteries added to her problems. When enough oxygen reached her brain, she'd be her old self for a short time. But as years passed, she grew more and more senile.

One day Rev. Horner brought his brother, who was visiting, to call on Mother. It was one of her very good days and she was suddenly the gracious hostess she'd always been. When my brother came she was able to perform the introductions and mentioned how much she was enjoying their visit.

An hour later she looked at Doc and asked, "Who're you?" How it hurt to see our sweet, brilliant mother begin to leave us.

Searching for Solutions

Doc's wife Hanne stayed with Mother while I worked. When I got home, I took over. But Mother began sleeping more and more during the day and then roaming the house at night, so even that arrangement proved impossible.

Once early in this period, she apparently dreamt that she was preparing dinner. Using her walker, she wandered into the kitchen in the middle of the night. She found apples and a sharp knife and returned to her room to begin peeling apples.

Something woke me and when I looked in on her, I was confronted with a huge bowl of rapidly browning apples. So at three o'clock in the morning, after a long day at work and very little sleep, I baked a pie and froze several others.

But such episodes were not always so innocent.

In the middle of a hard winter freeze, I fought my way up from a deep sleep to hear Trish weakly whining about being cold, asking me to hand her the extra blanket on the bottom of my bed. When I tried to rise, I felt as if I were moving through water. All I wanted was to lie down and go back to sleep.

Thankfully her pleas were insistent and some reserve of mothering instinct took over. I finally realized the room was filled with gas. Much to Trish's horror, instead of the blanket, I stumbled to the window by her bed and threw it open. Then I pulled her and her bedcovers over and made her stand there until our teeth were chattering and we were both wide awake.

Apparently Mom had decided to cook something again. She'd turned on the jets for the oven and all four burners, but had failed to light them. The only thing that saved us was that, on her way back to bed, she'd also shut off the furnace and turned our cozy little home into an icehouse.

After that, Doc put a lock on the kitchen door high enough to be out of Mother's reach. I used it at night or if I had to be gone for a few minutes. One Saturday Mother was lying down so I ran up the street to get some meat out of the locker we rented from a cold storage business in the middle of the block.

I returned to find neighbors herding Mother back in the house. She'd taken her walker out the front door, down the steps and headed toward the back to get into the locked kitchen. After that I didn't dare leave her alone for even a moment.

It Never Rains That It Doesn't Pour

We tried hiring women to stay with Mother at night but none lasted long. I caught one drinking. Small items went missing whenever another one had been on duty. Life was rapidly becoming a nightmare. And in the midst of all this, Trish came down with an illness that had been all but eradicated in the U.S.

It took six days for her symptoms to progress far enough to be recognized by our doctor, who'd thankfully been practicing since the days when such diseases were common. By then she'd endured an agonizingly painful throat, four ineffective shots of penicillin and nightly temperature elevations in the 104° range.

My contribution to all this was to remain awake each night, dividing my time between fighting Trish's fever peaks and keeping Mom from wandering out of the house in her birthday suit.

The only bright moment that entire week occurred because Trish reread one of her favorite books, *Mrs. Mike* by Benedict and Nancy Freedman. At one point in the novel, the Yukon-based heroine's children succumb to a diphtheria epidemic.

On Wednesday of her confinement, my ever-imaginative daughter tried to convince me that her symptoms exactly mimicked those of the children in the book. Knowing she'd been vaccinated for diphtheria as a child, I dismissed her self-diagnosis.

By the time we met Dr. Gehres in his office on Saturday (this is what is meant by the good old days), Trish was so weak I had to practically carry her into the examination room. He looked at her throat again, then frowned and gave one of those non-informative "mmm"s doctors seem to love.

He then went down the hall toward his pharmacy, but left the door ajar. We heard him dial the phone and then say, "This is Dr. Gehres. Do you have any diphtheria antitoxin on hand?"

At that point my gravely ill daughter, who only moments before could barely hold her head up, raised up on one elbow, focused her glazed eyes on mine and said, "I told you so."

It's easy to see why she chose to pen something as dramatic as suspense novels when she began her writing career.

A Heartbreaking Announcement

Life is never easy with three generations of a family living together. Throw in senility and add the presence of another adult (my brother) with a differing viewpoint on child raising and a once happy home can become a battlefield.

In addition to being a joint care giver for Mother, I was forced to act as a buffer between my daughter and my straight laced brother. Before, I had always been available when Trish needed me. Now I was constantly exhausted and rarely had time for the long talks we had always enjoyed. After five years of living in what had essentially become an extremely understaffed nursing home, our formerly relaxed dinner conversations had been replaced by tense confrontations like this:

Trish: "Can Barbara and Mary Ann sleep over Friday night?"
Me: "I don't think that's a good idea with Grandmother the way she is."
Trish: "Then what about just Barbara?"
Doc: "Your mother said no."
Trish: "Please, Mom?"
Doc: "Don't argue with your Mother."
Me: "It's okay, Doc."
Doc: "No, it's not okay. It's disrespectful."
Me: "Doc, please. Let me handle this."
Trish: "I don't see why I can't have anyone over to my house anymore."
Doc: "This is not *your* house. You're only living here through the kindness of your grandmother."

Of course, at this point Trish would flee the dinner table, get in her car and drive as far away as she could. And I would bite my tongue to keep from reminding my brother that for years, every time I'd discussed finding a library job and moving somewhere else, Mother had suddenly developed some new ailment. Now her problems were valid and I was trapped by my original decision as a widow to rely on my family.

I'd always encouraged Trish to be independent. She'd begun working at Murphy's Five and Dime when she turned sixteen and later moved to J. C. Penney's. Most of her pay went toward records and gas, although she did save a little. Now I began slipping her extra money so she could eat dinner at a drive-in where one of her best friends worked. From then on, the only time she came home was to change clothes and just before the curfew I'd assigned, when she knew Doc would be gone.

Inevitably, living this way pushed us even further apart and just before the end of her senior year and several months shy of her eighteenth birthday, Trish and her boyfriend Jerry came to ask for my permission to marry. When I asked, they admitted that there was a baby on the way.

Because of her youth I suggested she might like to think of other possibilities. But both were committed to the marriage. So Trish and Jerry Skillman were married on November 5, 1960, in the First Christian Church by Rev. Horner.

Like all mothers I wanted only the best for my child. But after the initial shock, I realized I'd done my best. I couldn't live my child's life. Some things must be learned the hard way.

After all those years of needing a man in her life, she'd decided Jerry was the one. And I have to admit that she knew her own mind. In the years since then I've watched them bond and grow in wisdom and maturity. Jerry's love healed a painful place in her heart and I know I could not have had a better or sweeter and more wonderful son-in-law. I have loved him like a son.

As I write this, almost forty years have gone by. She and Jerry have raised two beautiful and productive children and are still happily married. He spoils her (when he's not busy spoiling their granddaughter) and supported one hundred and ten percent her decision to quit a twenty-five year banking career to live her dream of becoming a published writer.

What more could any mother ask?

My Sister's Marriage

Shortly after Dad's death, Lowene had married Joe, her long time suitor. Joe was a district manager for a wine and liquor distributer when they met, and much later a real estate broker for business properties. He was also a perfectionist whom Lowene later realized needed to control everything around him.

While they were courting, Joe was charming and generous, bringing her flowers and small items for the little two-bedroom house she'd purchased when the Depression ended. It was not until many years later that I learned he became abusive once they were married. Unfortunately, such situations were rarely discussed in those days, even within families, so none of us recognized what are now the classic signs of abuse.

Joe was Catholic, but his parents were divorced. He told Lowene that his father had abused his mother and once locked Joe in a hen house for a minor mistake. Joe had also been briefly married and divorced. He had little use for children and I think, with his need for control, saw my lonely, barren sister as the perfect solution to his church's edict against birth control.

Although Lowene agreed to honor his religion and its dietary restrictions, she made it clear she'd remain a protestant. She couldn't accept the tenet that one could sin, be absolved by a priest and then continually repeat the cycle. Her conviction was reinforced when Joe would abuse her, go to confession, gain forgiveness, and then turn right around and mistreat her again. Despite this, Joe harassed her constantly to convert.

Although we disliked the mean-spirited teasing and cutting remarks Joe often directed at Lowene in our presence, coming from a close-knit family blinded us to the possibility that my beloved sister might be going through hell when we weren't around. Only when I spent a extended period with them at their retirement home in Arizona after Lowene was injured in a car accident did I glimpse the true nature of their relationship.

Painful Hindsight

I realize now that Lowene might have remained in her abusive relationship because of her low self-esteem. Love was the first child whom Mom welcomed with joy. Doc was the favored son. I was the baby. Lowene, whose birth had ended mother's quest for a degree, never quite fit. With all her wonderful qualities, Mom's inability to recognize what her indifference was doing to my sister amazes me.

It's not that Mom was intentionally cruel. On the contrary, in most situations, she treated all of us equally. I, certainly, never felt unloved. Her prejudice against Lowene manifested itself more in her unconscious dismissal of my more timid sister's feelings. The following episode that I witnessed is a good example.

Mother had taken my sisters to a department store in Indianapolis before Love returned for her sophomore year at Michigan and Lowene entered as a freshman. This was a major event before malls and specialty shops on almost every corner. Traveling to the city meant train tickets and departure deadlines.

Love, who was easy to fit, had a keen sense of style and an eye for fashion. Mom found shopping with her a joy. Lowene, however, was extremely petite, barely four eleven and small-boned. Buying for her was a nightmare of searching through girl's size clothing for things with enough sophistication for an adult.

To Mom, price was also a factor, so in addition to enjoying Love's delight at modeling all the newest styles, she spent extra time evaluating each purchase. Knowing their time was limited, Lowene asked to go alone to her own department and do her own shopping. But Love insisted they needed a third opinion. Since Lowene had a good eye for value, Love had a point.

Still, by the time Mom deemed Love's wardrobe purchases complete, there was very little time left to shop for Lowene. Rather than make an issue of the situation or rush through her own choices and regret them later, Lowene said she'd make do with the things she already had.

After they returned, Mother was eager to show Dad what good bargains she found. Love, who was naturally excited, opened box after box, pointing out various fashion features as she modeled their purchases. When the last box had been opened, Dad turned to Lowene and asked her where her things were.

I give my sister credit for hiding her disappointment. Lowene didn't whine. She simply murmured that there hadn't been enough time and assured him she really didn't need that much anyway. My father, whom I realize now was never oblivious to such incidents, promptly declared that everyone needed new things when they were beginning a college career. He told her he was going to take her on another shopping trip himself.

He and Lowene spent hours in the same Indianapolis department store. But where Mom sought out fashions with bargain prices, Dad believed that you got what you paid for and that quality lasted longer. As a result, Lowene's traditionally fashionable wardrobe took her through both her university days and her early years as a working woman.

By itself, the above episode might seem an isolated incident. Indeed, not until I was older and away from the day-to-day pressures of family living did the impact of the accumulation of dozens such experiences throughout the formative period of my sister's life begin to emerge. By then, it was much to late to undo the damage to Lowene's self-esteem.

A Final Confession

In the Spring of 1960 Mother began bleeding internally and was admitted to the hospital. For a while she lingered, lucid now and then, but more often confused and unable to respond. Near the end, I asked if there was anything I could get her. She shook her head, then suddenly opened her eyes, squeezed my hand, and said quite clearly, "I didn't do right by Lowene."

Those were her last words to me before she fell into a coma and died on March 28, 1961. I can only believe that her statement was her way of making peace with God before he took her home. If only the rest of us could have known such closure in the days ahead.

Settling the Estate

With both our parents now gone, it was time for we four children to pay the piper.

Over time, Dad's investment in the farms had grown and both properties were now worth a great deal. But Mother, as Dad had before her, died without a will. No one questioned the decision to settle our outstanding college debts to our various siblings out of our shares from selling the farms. But conflict arose when we began discussing what Lowene had loaned Dad.

During the depression years, in addition to helping both Doc and me through college, Lowene had kept Dad from losing the farms by paying taxes and other critical expenses. By the time Dad recovered from his economic woes the war was on. Then he died before he could erase the debt.

Perhaps, given enough time and without interference, we could have worked through the problems of deciding a fair division of the estate. But just as there had been no wills drawn up, the written agreements concerning Dad's debt to Lowene had not addressed the subject of interest. No one, least of all Lowene, had expected the balance to remain unpaid for so long.

This wasn't a major issue to Lowene, but when Joe insisted she was owed interest - at an excessive rate - for all the years our debt and Dad's had remained partially unpaid, the die was cast.

Eventually, compromises were made all around. But the bitter taste Joe injected into the situation poisoned forever the loving relationships between the remaining members of the Barnett family. After the settlement, Love and Doc had little to do with Lowene. But she'd done too much for me over the years for me to abandon her completely.

I think my other siblings thought Lowene should have shut Joe out of what we all considered internal family negotiations. And perhaps they were right. But I also doubt either of them ever realized the true nature of the relationship between Lowene and her husband. If they had, things might have been different.

Many years later, after Lowene's death, the rest of us got back together, but we were never again the harmonious family we had once been. Nothing could heal the heartache and hurt feelings nor erase the suffering Joe had caused.

Right: Frances Macdonald fixing hotdogs for hungry teens, New Year's Eve 1959

Below: Patricia Macdonald with her car, c. 1959

Cora Barnett and Frances Macdonald, as Cora's health was failing, c. 1960

Patricia Macdonald senior photo 1961

Below: Frances Macdonald with first grandchild Pamela Michelle Skillman, c. 1962

Above: Patricia and Jerry Skillman, November 5, 1960

Pamela Skillman, age 4, c. 1965

Frances Macdonald's grandson Jeffrey Hale Skillman, age 2, c. 1965

NINETEEN

A LIBRARIAN AGAIN

My first grandchild was born June 9, 1961, an adorable little red-haired, blue-eyed baby whom Trish and Jerry named Pamela Michelle. One look at that child and my world became a happy place once again.

After Mother died, I continued to live in the house on Hendricks Street and work at the church. But in the summer of 1962 I applied for a position at the Indiana State Library in Indianapolis. I was fifty-one and had been away from my profession for over twenty years, but when I interviewed with Hazel Hopper in the Indiana Division for a position as a manuscript librarian, I knew I'd found my niche.

Working in the Indiana Division offered variety and challenge because the division's collection was unique. Personal papers of congressmen, state legislators, authors and average citizens with connections to the state had been collected, as had books by Indiana authors and any work written about the Hoosier state. Years of newspapers, clippings and picture files had been indexed and a card index had been designed to reference it all.

Waiting on the public was a big challenge until I learned the collection, but cataloging new manuscript material was fun and interesting.

Leaving Shelbyville

Driving to and from work, seventy miles each day, proved more exhausting than I'd expected. As winter came, driving ice-covered roads was also difficult. Mother's house would be sold eventually, so I began to look for a rental home in Indianapolis.

My first place was a nice double on the southeast side near Ellenberger Park where Hanne and I had often taken our children while visiting her aunt. Now it was Pam who played on the park's pumpkin-colored metal Cinderella coach and stone horses.

Eight months after I moved, the owner died and the house was sold. Despite my year's lease, I was given two weeks to leave. With Jerry and Trish's help I moved into another double, on Audubon Street. This place was near several eating places and closer to the bus line for snowy days. I really liked the house until winter arrived and the owners refused to fix the faulty furnace.

I was still living there when my second grandchild Jeffrey Hale Skillman was born August 29, 1963. But soon after that, the area began to change and I decided it was time to move on. Not far away, I discovered a nice neighborhood of new construction within walking distance of three bus lines. So in 1964 I moved into my own small three bedroom ranch home.

Gathering Material

Part of my responsibilities were to collect letters, documents and other manuscripts with a connection to Indiana. Many collections were brought in by the owners, but sometimes we had to go to the source to evaluate what was being offered and make a bid based on the importance to our collection. Often this took me far from Indianapolis, as when I was sent to Washington D.C. to look over the Congressional papers of Rep. Ralph Harvey

I'd never flown, so I was excited as well as a bit apprehensive about the trip. Several of Harvey's staff took me to dinner at Trader Vic's the evening I arrived. The next day I met Rep. Harvey, looked over the material and made arrangements to ship the collection to the library. After having lunch with the representative and several of his colleagues, I took a quick tour of the Capital and I left that same evening.

I accomplished quite a bit in that day and a half.

Library Adventures

Many people believe the traditional myth that working in a library is unexciting. But between naive and criminal patrons, I found library life anything but dull.

Anyone who's ever attempted to trace their family tree knows that genealogy is usually a lifelong job. Anyone, that is, except one Indianapolis policeman who read a newspaper article about finding your family's roots and dropped by the State Library. His request had us in stitches for weeks:

"I want to trace my family's history. I'm parked in a 15 minute zone, so that's all the time I can spare." He just couldn't believe his family genealogy wasn't all ready and waiting to be picked up.

In our division a doctor once asked to see our county histories, which contained biographical material about the early settlers in each county. After he left, we discovered several columns neatly cut out of the book he'd been using. The next time he came in, he asked for a different county history.

Although the secretary we had watching him couldn't catch him defacing the material, a patron saw him use a scalpel to cut something out and a security guard was summoned. The man admitted vandalism and was later discovered to be mentally ill. We had to replace the mutilated pages with copies from another collection.

I missed the department's biggest confrontation with a criminal, because I was on vacation. But the episode was unique enough to bear retelling.

A professor and his pregnant wife, the Stanhopes, came to use the manuscripts. We were short handed and no one could stay with them constantly. Every time he was given the collection he'd asked for, he requested another, sending the librarian back to the vault. During all this, his pregnant wife kept using the restroom. By the time the pair left, the staff was worn out.

Several weeks later the FBI informed us that the same couple had been caught trying to sell stolen materials from another collection to a private Detroit library. A search of their home and car had turned up material from various other libraries, including our own.

The man's name was not Stanhope, nor was he a professor. His wife had not been pregnant, but had worn a dress with a hidden pouch where she stashed the letters they were stealing. In addition, they had abandoned their four children in Indiana.

Mrs. Hopper was flown to Detroit to testify and to try to identify our material. Thanks to the completeness of our unique card system, she was able to establish our claim. Unfortunately, other libraries were not so lucky. As a result, the judge ruled that any unidentified material would become our property as well.

The Detroit hotel where the FBI housed Mrs. Hopper turned out to be the same one in which my Mafia neighbor had been killed some thirty years before. Sometimes it really is a small world.

If You Can't Stand the Heat . . .

Our Library was not air conditioned and the heat and humidity was harmful to our books, especially in the stacks where there were no windows. Every year, our budget request for air conditioning was cut by the state legislature.

One unusually hot summer day the outside temperature was 108°. In our stacks where no air circulated it was nearer 120°. The only air moving came from one small fan which we kept turned toward the librarians' desks. Into this situation came the governor's wife to do some research.

She sat at a table and began working with the material that the librarians brought her. First she removed a bracelet and necklace and dropped them in her purse. Next she took off her jacket. Then she put a Kleenex tissue under her arm and kept wiping her face because of the perspiration.

One of the boys retrieving books in the stacks was overcome by the heat. Someone helped him to a chair, turned the fan on him and then ran for a glass of water. Someone else brought in wet towels to help cool him off.

The governor's wife asked what had happened. So, of course, we gave her a detailed description of what it was like in those 120° stacks. That coming year funds were appropriated from the governor's contingency fund to install air conditioning in the state library.

Good Friends and Good Fun

When I'd first begun working in Indianapolis, I was so worn down from caring for Mother that what began as a bad cold turned to pneumonia. Although the doctor poured enough antibiotics into me to, as he so eloquently put it, "cure syphilis," I couldn't shake off the effects. Finally, I took a leave of absence and drove to New Orleans with Rose Ann Johnson and another friend to sit in the sun. Within a week I stopped coughing.

That trip was the beginning of many excursions Rose Ann or other friends and I would take over the years. At various times I saw the Canadian Rockies, Banff and Lake Louise and the Dakotas and other neighboring states.

In Jasper, Canada a noise roused Rosie very early one morning. When she glanced out the window, she quickly shook our friend Nancy and me awake. Fourteen elk and deer were drinking at the stream behind our cabin. A mist had risen and moonlight was illuminating a beautiful tableau that still lingers in my mind.

We were always hoping to catch a glimpse of bears on these outings. Once an old timer told us we needed to go to the town dump right after the evening garbage had been discarded, so we drove out and parked next to an outhouse and then waited. And waited and waited. When it began to rain, we sought momentary cover in the outhouse.

"For my vacation there's nothing I like better than standing in a smelly outhouse at a town dump in the pouring rain waiting for some damn bears to show up," Rosie muttered.

Just then two big grizzlies waddled out and started eating the garbage. Suddenly Momma bear, who'd been looking towards the woods, raised her head and we saw a wolverine slinking around. Momma got down on all fours and lumbered after it, but Poppa just kept on eating. Some might call it an absurd adventure, but we sure wound up with a great memory.

I had a second encounter with bears, this time black ones, when Dorothy Riker, a librarian from another division, and I drove to the Smokies for a week's vacation. One day while hiking on a marked trail in the park, I heard something moving ahead and picked up a hefty stick for protection.

We slowly advanced and came upon a momma and three cubs eating berries. I glanced at Dorothy and saw that the defensive weapon she'd chosen was a tree limb so large both of us together couldn't have raised it as a shield. Thankfully, rather than attack, momma bear lumbered off with her three little ones humping along behind her.

When we told a park ranger about the three cubs, we learned that ours was the first verification of the rumored triplets he'd received.

More Library Tales

As my work load increased, we hired a young field agent named Tom Krasean to travel and find new sources. Often Tom and I went out to go through manuscripts together. If an owner didn't want to sell their historical material outright, we would ask permission to microfilm it with a portable machine we carried with us. I arranged and dated the material and Tom copied it.

The first time Tom and I had to copy a large collection, we had to stay overnight. Although there was quite a difference in our ages and we always stayed in separate rooms, Tom would later tease me by calling me his roommate.

At one home where we copied some Civil War letters, the elderly Mormon woman insisted that we take lunch with her. Tom liked the homemade pickles she served and almost ate the whole jar. Later, we were especially glad the woman had contacted us when she did. A few months after we filmed her material, we learned she'd passed away. Many wonderful collections such as hers are lost forever because heirs often don't realize the historical value of the material.

Mrs. Hopper also hired a woman named Claudia, the wife of an FBI agent who'd been transferred to Indianapolis. Claudia, a beautiful girl with dimpled cheeks, was from Georgia and her thick southern accent captivated us all. College students wanted her to wait on them just to hear her voice.

Ferne Roseman and Hazel Hopper and I were known as the Leos because we all shared the same astrological sign. One day our horoscope read we should leave our work to others. Because many of the staff were off that day, we showed Claudia the warning.

She reacted exactly as we hoped, treating us to an indignant, "If y'all think I'm gonna do all the work around here, y'all have another think comin'!" When that Georgia accent sent us into hysterics, she realized we'd been teasing. She was a good sport to put up with us all.

Groups I Enjoyed

I led a busy life with my work and various club memberships and two grandchildren to love, baby sit and entertain.

When I first moved to Indianapolis I was asked to join the International Travel Study Club, a large organization with chapters in Canada and several Caribbean Islands. Each month our Woodruff Chapter met in one of its members' homes to hear well-educated guest speakers discuss destinations they'd traveled to or sometimes simply researched extensively.

At various times I held each of the elected offices in the chapter - president, vice-president, secretary, treasurer, and phone and program chairs. At one time we had over forty members and usually met at restaurants with private dining rooms.

Another club I joined was the Naptown Snappers, a group of would-be photographers whose only membership requirement was ownership of 35mm camera and a home in which to serve dessert for at least one monthly meeting a year. Most of us took slides, so I purchased a screen and projector.

While many of the members' pictures were of spring and fall foliage or scenes of winter, mine were of Canada, the Smokey Mountains, or my trips to the eastern and western United States and, eventually, Europe. I also included places and events I visited in Indiana such as the Covered Bridge Festival that is held every year in Parke County.

TWENTY

A GRAND MEMORY

In 1972 Dorothy Riker and I planned a trip to Europe. Shortly before we were to leave, I noticed that whenever I approached a group at work, everyone fell silent or just disappeared. I was hurt by the way they avoided my company and began to wonder if I had suddenly developed body odor or something equally offensive.

The weekend before my departure, Rose Ann and her friend Alice Carpenter took me out to dinner. I thought nothing about Rosie's suggestion that we run by their apartment for a moment. Her insistence that we stop to see the complex's newly decorated party room seemed a bit strange, at least until I went in and a room full of friends and family shouted "Surprise!"

Rosie and Alice had reserved and decorated the room, then left Trish and Jerry and another surprise - Lowene and her husband - to greet the guests while they took me to dinner.

I nearly fainted when I saw all the people. I looked at my coworkers and said, "This is why you avoided me." They admitted they'd been afraid they'd spoil the surprise. Several people such as Frances Ober, my best friend from high school, and Rev. Horner had been unable to attend but sent tapes wishing me Bon Voyage.

Trish had gone to my house on her day off a few weeks before and spirited away extra plates and tablecloths for the party, as well as dozens of photos from old albums that she used to create a "This Is Your Life" memory book. Clever little detective that she was, I'd never even suspected she'd been in the house.

The Ultimate Trip

My grand tour of Europe was the dream of a lifetime. While only a small blip in my vast store of accumulated memories, the images are still vivid. Those for whom travelogues are not preferred reading consider yourselves forewarned.

Dorothy and I and about fifty others from various places began our tour by flying to New York, then on to London where we took in all the ususal sights, even catching a glimpse of the queen when she passed by and waved. Even almost thirty years after the war, parts of London were still being restored.

From there we flew to Amsterdam where bicycles were residents' preferred mode of transportation. Narrow, three and four story homes with large upper windows fronted the canals. Boxes vivid with late-blooming flowers adorned each balcony.

We learned that the stairs in those homes were so narrow that furniture could not be carried up. Instead, at the peak of each roof, a rope and pulley attached to a long support beam was used to pull large items up to the various floors, where the furniture was then swung through one of the oversized windows.

Other vivid memories from our Holland stop are the annex where Ann Frank and her family lived in hiding from the Nazis and a windmill surrounded by a profusion of tulips.

While the majority of our group toured a diamond factory, Dorothy and I visited the Ryka Museum to view the work of the Dutch Masters. We expected to be picked up by late afternoon but had to wait until almost dinner before the bus finally came.

It seems the owners of the diamond factory had locked our tour group in the display room and refused to let them out until someone bought something. Finally one couple bought some earrings and everyone was permitted to leave.

After a stop at the Hague we went to Brussels, then entered West Germany and boarded a boat and floated down the Rhine past vineyard-covered terraced hillsides and small towns perched on the slopes. Now and then we spotted a castle. Towns in Germany are close so we were able to visit several in a day, making such stops as Ludwig Von Beethoven's house in Bonn.

The Grand Tour Continues

At the urging of several in our group, we detoured to Berlin, which wasn't on our original itinerary. As we drove along the Berlin wall, we caught glimpses of the watch towers and Soviet guards every so often. We stopped near the entryway from West to East. The West Berlin guards, while serious looking, had pleasant expressions. The Soviet guards were very grim.

From Berlin, we drove to Rothenberg then to Munich where we saw the stadium from the 1936 Olympics where Jessie Owen had given Hitler a good lesson in superiority. We also had a typical meal of wienerschnizel and potatoes at a local beer hall. After dinner, the Germans sang songs, some of which were probably bawdy, but since I'd forgotten most of my college German I caught only a word or two here and there.

From Munich we went to Austria to visit Mozart's birth place and then on to Vienna where we took walks along the Danube River. Our hotel was across from a tea or coffee house where a continental orchestra played everything from "The Blue Danube" to classical and semi-classical music and even American jazz. We spent several afternoons there, listening and enjoying tortes and other treats.

One day we visited the Spanish Riding Stable and Academy where Lippizaner horses were trained. Although the original group that had been saved from destruction from the Nazis were on tour, we watched them train a younger horse.

From Vienna we crossed the Alps where we could view the Matterhorn, then entered Yugoslavia, the only Communist country on our thirty day tour.

Inside the Iron Curtain

At the border our passports were collected. When a guard handed them back, he checked our faces against our photos very carefully. Our guide had warned us to be careful in our remarks. Once cleared to enter the country, we drove to our hotel in Bled.

We were instructed not to talk to the waiters or other personnel. The hotel was on a lovely small lake. Our rooms were clean but very plain with coarse toilet paper, like a fine sandpaper. We'd been warned and brought our own.

The private dining room our group had been assigned had one waiter for every five or six people. Ours was very young and eager to learn English. As he served he would point to my purse and say, "Vhat is?" I whispered back, "Purse or pocket book," and he would repeat the words. Then he touched my blouse, my watch and the water glass so he could learn those words as well. All of us were being asked questions. So much for not speaking to the help. Even our maid and housekeeper talked to us.

Italy

From Bled we drove over the Alps and down into Italy. We reached Venice in the afternoon and took a gondola ride through canals filled with debris and garbage. After dinner it began to rain and the romantic gondola ride with singing gondoliers that we'd planned didn't appeal so much anymore. The next morning at the Murano glass factory I bought a simple blue vase to complement a Delft vase I bought in Holland. Both now sit in the bay window of my apartment.

St. Mark's Square Basilica was filled with pigeons and gulls which the Venetians were constantly trying to discourage since it's difficult to drink coffee with birds flying overhead.

The next morning we left for Florence, the art cultural city of Italy. I'd really enjoyed my college art appreciation course, but had never expected to view the real pieces. There is no way one can see or even begin to describe all the beautiful art treasures of Florence. From there we went to Rome where we saw Vatican City. Although restoration scaffolding in the Sistine Chapel blocked part of the view, the sections that had already been cleaned were truly unbelievable.

Dorothy and I and two other women made a point one night of visiting a little side street restaurant where the locals ate. Although the Maitre D did not speak English, one of the other patrons who did translated their specialty which proved to be delicious. That evening we felt we'd seen the real Italy.

From Rome we drove to Naples where our guide was a funny little man who must have been a school teacher, since he treated us like children. Naples had narrow streets with laundry strung over almost every alley and street. Mount Vesuvius loomed over the city and one of our stops was the excavation of Pompeii.

Over the Alps

The next morning we started toward Switzerland, stopping to see the leaning tower of Pisa and passing through Nice and Cannes (where the big film festival is now held) and Monaco where we saw the Grimaldi's palace and the casino in Monte Carlo. The gambling there was too fast for me. Some of the group tried to get in a game, but the stakes were too high.

After seeing Geneva and Lausanne, we entered Switzerland's capital of Bern, noted for its clock tower's architecture and figurines and tunes. Our next stop was Zurich, a commercial town with a beautiful lake dotted with sail boats.

En route to Paris the main road was closed for repairs and our route of secondary roads was rough - few towns and even fewer restrooms. It was murder for a bus load of women. At one restroom break, our driver kept apologizing profusely before we even left the bus. Entering the rest area, we understood why.

The facility was a hole in the cement and a rope on a pulley which you pulled to flush. Squatting in the bushes couldn't have been much more primitive, but everyone made the best of the situation. I emerged to find some shocked young girls hesitating outside. I told them, "Now, if an old lady like me can do it, so can you." At that point I'd have gladly welcomed that smelly old Canadian outhouse where I waited in the rain for the bears.

Because of the construction detour, we reached Paris late at night. Our driver thought that buses were forbidden on the avenue in front of the hotel, so he drove on side streets.

Three times parked cars kept him from maneuvering those narrow lanes, but he simply commandeered some of the local young men who gathered on almost every corner to lift the VW bugs and other small vehicles onto the sidewalk so we could pass. Then he made sure the cars were replaced and tipped the boys who'd helped. Eventually, we reached our hotel.

That next day we saw the sights, strolled the Champs Elysees and watched student artists along the Seine. In the Louvre Museum we had to pay to use the restroom. After the previous day's ordeal, paying for modern facilities didn't seem quite as unreasonable as it might have.

On our free day Dorothy and I spent a busman's holiday at the Paris Library and National Archives, took a boat ride on the Seine, and had an early dinner. When we returned to the hotel, Paris was aglow, illustrating its reputation as the city of lights.

Walking through the gardens in Luxembourg the next day, we rested for a few minutes on one of the benches. Suddenly an attendant appeared and informed us that if we sat, we had to pay. Rather than protest we paid, then promptly left. Bathrooms are one thing. Paying to enjoy sunshine and fresh air is another.

After a farewell dinner in Paris, we said goodbye to our German driver. At the airport, I had very little to declare, since I'd sent many of my purchases home to Trish. After thirty wonderful, exhausting days, it was good to get back to Indy and my own bed.

The "Leos"
Fern Roseman, Frances Macdonald,
Hazel Hopper, an unidentified friend,
and Dorothy Riker, June 10, 1990

Frances Macdonald's Bon Voyage party
July 16, 1971. *Left to Right:* Jerry and
Trish Skillman, Frances, Alice
Carpenter, and Rose Ann Johnson

Left: Frances Macdonald
plays Cupid at her India-
napolis home for grandson
Jeffrey Skillman and Jay
Velgos' first "meet my
family" visit, April 1992

Pat Page (Fern's daughter),
Jeffrey Skillman, Jay Velgos, Frances
Macdonald, and Fern Roseman,
outside a favorite restaurant,
April 1992

Frances Macdonald reading to great-granddaugher RaBecca Bartee, probably age 3-4, c. 1996

RaBecca Bartee, age 4-5, in Papaw and Nana's Wichita Falls redbud, c. 1997

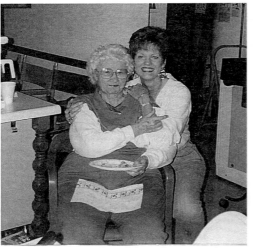

Frances Macdonald at the surprise "moving to Texas" party given by Judy, her long-time hairdresser in Indianapolis, April 1995

Frances Macdonald at her Rolling Meadows apartment in Wichita Falls, TX. Birdhouse was going away gift from Judy, her Indianapolis hairdresser. April 1995

TWENTY-ONE

WELCOMING THE NEXT PHASE OF MY LIFE

After my European trip, life settled down to an everyday routine. On weekends I visited Trish and sometimes took the grandchildren to historical places in Indiana.

Every year the State Library and the Historical Society sponsored a joint history conference from a Friday through Sunday usually at various lodges throughout our state parks. Speakers included authors or professors. One archaeologist told of his recent digs and spoke on the history of Indians in Indiana.

I was asked to speak about the Indiana Division's work, especially about how we found manuscripts. I survived and even answered questions at one large gathering but once was enough.

Many of my friends liked to travel but didn't drive, so when I wanted to go somewhere, I simply called a few and always found someone willing to accompany me.

Some of the historical places in Indiana I took my grandchildren were Lincoln's boyhood cabin, and Vincennes and Corydon, the first and second state capitals before the government was moved to Indianapolis.

On other trips we went caving and visited Santa Claus Land, many of the state parks, and the restored French settlement in Vincennes. We also followed the Lincoln trail to Lincoln's home in Illinois and then toured the Illinois State Capitol building.

Family Travels

In 1975 Jerry and Trish and Pam and Jeff and I drove to Philadelphia. We'd decided that the next year's bicentennial crowds (and raised prices) would make such a visit much less enjoyable. Except for some in-progress building restorations and road construction, we had a wonderful time.

At the time there were few family eating places available in the historical area where we'd booked our hotel. Feeding a family of five in the hotel's dining room proved very expensive, so one evening we decided to find a Bonanza Steak House for dinner.

The address on the map we consulted didn't seem that far away and one street seemed the most direct route, so off we went. Unfortunately we got a good view of the seamier side of the City of Brotherly Love. As we drove down the street we saw women carrying baseball bats or accompanied by huge dogs on heavy chain leashes. We decided it might be better to plot a different route for our return when it would be much later.

After our inexpensive dinner, we again consulted the map. This time our route involved a tangle of highways to negotiate and many confusing roads with missing street signs. Just when Jerry was sure we were on the right street, we found ourselves on a toll bridge into New Jersey. We were trapped in the left lane with cement barriers that prevented any attempt to turn off for miles on both sides of the bridge.

Finally, Jerry worked his way into the right lane and managed to turn off. But we still weren't home.

Choosing a different street (with another toll bridge, of course), he pulled into the line of cars and waited our turn at the booth. Because he wanted to get through quickly, he kept his window down and held the fifteen cent toll in his hand. Just as we were about to reach the booth, he dropped one of the coins.

By this time the kids were laughing hysterically. Trish and I weren't in much better shape. Eventually we found our way back to our hotel in downtown Philadelphia.

Thankfully, Jerry has a wonderful sense of humor and didn't mind all the teasing. He *did* reveal, however, that after being stationed at Fort Dix, New Jersey in the dead of winter during his National Guard training, he'd vowed never to return to that state.

Repeat Performance

I wish I could say that was the end of the entire New Jersey incident, but it wasn't. The next morning as we were leaving to drive to Gettysburg, we again encountered a maze of highways with confusing signs and once more became trapped on the way to Jerry's least favorite state.

Even with all our unplanned adventures we had a delightful trip. Jeff had become a big fan of Lincoln and was impressed to stand on the same spot where the President had delivered his Gettysburg Address. We also located the battlefield monument for my great-grandfather's 82nd Ohio regiment.

Later we visited Strasbourg, PA where we rode the train that had been used in the movie "Hello Dolly" and saw the Amish in their plain clothes and black buggies. We also got a chance to taste the wonderful Pennsylvania Dutch and Amish cooking. A side trip to Hershey gave the children a chance to see the unique streetlights shaped like chocolate and foiled-wrapped kisses.

A Changing of the Guard

Soon after our family trip, Hazel Hopper decided to retire. Reluctantly, I agreed to take her place as head of the division. Of course, as soon as I said yes, a long hoped for library addition became a reality. The air conditioning construction had been a mess, but it was nothing compared to such a major remodeling.

Computers were still fairly new in the mid 1970s. We'd been hooked up with Indiana University by computer for some time, but it seemed as if the system was down for longer periods than it was up and running. Because of that and the unique nature of our historical documents, many of us in the department resisted the idea of discarding the informative card system that had proved itself over and over through the years.

I realized we were fighting a losing battle and decided it was time to retire.

As I looked back over my years at the library, I realized I had served under five different library directors and at least four different Governors. I had hoped to retire quietly, but the girls in the division gave me a retirement tea. It was quite lovely and I was glad I'd not protested too much.

Volunteer Work

After awhile I became bored, so friends suggested I volunteer at the Methodist Hospital. As a Pink Lady, I sorted incoming cards and letters. With skills I'd developed during years of deciphering handwritten manuscripts, I found the work less frustrating than others might have.

Working as a Pink Lady led to another volunteer position with the Quaker Guild, which rolled burn dressings. Because our hand-rolled versions were much softer, both doctors and patients preferred them to the commercial ones the hospital purchased.

Unfortunately, many of the group are now gone or too ill to work. As a result, the Quaker Guild has been disbanded. I keep in touch with the Guild's former treasurer and it saddens me to hear of the toll the years have taken on my old friends.

Retirement Trips

I did a lot of domestic traveling after I retired. Rose Ann and Alice and a woman named Claire and I especially enjoyed one two-week trip in the U.S. Rocky Mountains.

We donned helmets and descended into an old gold mine in Victor, Colorado where to our surprise we encountered fellow adventurer Walter Cronkite. Our most unique stop may well have been in Cripple Creek, where the city had restored, with the help of an aging former lady of the evening, one of its many bordellos.

In Durango we rode the narrow gauge railroad to Silverton in a coach with open windows. At Telluride the driver of a Jeep excursion took us to the very edge of the mountain for a breathtaking view. Then, in Ouray as we came down off the mountain at dusk, we sat at an overlook and watched the lights come on in the town below.

It was easy to understand why Colin loved mountains so. How I wished we could have shared those moments.

On the River

Trish and Jerry moved to Wichita Falls, Texas in 1980, but left Jeff with Jerry's parents so he could complete his senior year at Shelbyville. My loving grandson spent many weekends with me as well that year. Of course, I'll admit some of the attraction might have been my willingness to let him borrow my car now and then.

I felt the absence of my family keenly, but kept busy with my volunteer work and various trips. In 1981 the Historical Society sponsored a trip down the Ohio on the Delta Queen paddlewheel in celebration of the Society's 150th year.

I went as a substitute for someone who canceled. I enjoyed the leisurely journey into the past, but the woman who'd begged me to fill in had many friends aboard. After a brief "good morning," I never saw her until bed time. My friends on board all had spouses or cabin mates with which to share activities.

With the exception of the births of my grandchildren, I think I longed for Colin more then than at any other time. It made me wonder just how different my life might have been.

Reunions

Although I'd visited Trish and Jerry in Shelbyville often, I seldom went back for church. I did attend the 150th anniversary of the church's founding. It was good to see the three families I'd worked with so closely - Rev. and Mrs. Ford, John and Ellen Faust, and Jim and Emma Horner - together at the same time.

Another visit to the church was for Reverend Horner's retirement celebration. It was an afternoon for renewal of friendships. Trish was visiting from Texas at the time and was also able to see many old friends.

Making A Tough Decision

Wichita Falls is about nine hundred miles from Indianapolis and driving to visit Trish and Jerry and the children was becoming too much. My experience on the way back one year convinced me that long road trips - at least with me behind the wheel - were no longer an option.

I was nearing a rest area when a car driven by an elderly gentleman passed me. He realized that the exit ramp was almost upon him, so he cut across in front of my car, missing it by no more than an inch. His poor wife's face was chalk white. She looked so frightened I thought, if she was the one in need of the facility, it was probably too late to do her any good.

To avoid disaster, I'd swerved to my left and crossed the center line. Moments later it occurred to me that I could have been hit by another car. That realization was so frightening I pulled to the side of the road. Suddenly I began to shake. My heart was pounding wildly and I had trouble breathing.

Some time after this, my internist detected an irregular heartbeat. When I asked what might have caused this, she told me that such problems were often the result of a shock or emotional trauma. I mentioned my recent near-miss. Her response was emphatic, "From now on, you're flying."

As a precaution, I saw a heart specialist who suggested using electrical shock therapy to regulate my heart beat. Unfortunately, three separate attempts failed to restore a normal rhythm. The final prognosis was that I'd simply have to learn to live with the problem.

From then on, I restricted my driving to short trips around the Indianapolis area and flew to Texas for my visits.

The Hardest Blow of All

A few years after my heart episode, I noticed I was drifting toward the left whenever I drove and having difficulty seeing the center line. Despite previous cataract surgeries on both eyes and glaucoma medication, I was losing the sight in my left eye.

The diagnosis: macular degeneration in both eyes and a blood clot behind my left eye. After several failed attempts to correct the latter situation, my ophthalmologist was forced to admit defeat. Since I didn't want to endanger others, I realized it was time to restrict my driving even more.

Now my only times behind the wheel were short trips to the neighborhood drugstore or grocery and to my hairdresser's. I drove only during daylight hours, tried to schedule such trips for hours when traffic would be lightest and stayed in the right lane and watched the white stripe with my good right eye.

Martha Wright now assumed responsibility for driving Fern Roseman and me and herself to Hazel's for our standing Sunday luncheon outings. She also drove us to many evening events, often using my car which was larger than her own.

Around this same time, my doctor moved her office to the opposite side of Indianapolis. Taking a cab to her new office soon became very costly and I realized the time had come to look for a retirement environment that offered transportation.

Since I was so far away from Trish and the children, I felt I should choose a place closer to her. My great-granddaughter RaBecca was now on the scene as well, making such a move even more attractive.

The Meadows

During a visit with Jerry and Trish in March of 1994, I discussed my plans. My hope was to find a place that would allow me to live as independently as possible but would also offer more intensive care when that was no longer feasible. I remembered how bone weary I was after caring for Mother and had no intention of putting my family through a similar experience.

Although I wasn't quite ready to make a move, Trish suggested I visit Rolling Meadows, a retirement center in Wichita Falls. The marketing director, gave us a brochure with floor plans and pricing and took us on a tour.

Rolling Meadows offered exactly what I was looking for - three separate levels of retirement care: Independent Living in one, two, or three bedroom cottages or the atrium center's efficiency or one or two bedroom apartments; Carefree Living (CLU) apartments for those who were no longer self-sufficient but didn't require total nursing care on a daily basis; and a Health Care Center with private and semi-private rooms for those with the greatest need.

Located on several acres of beautifully landscaped grounds, it had a heated outside pool, library, beauty shop, fitness center, game room, chapel, and scheduled transportation to the grocery, the mall, and doctor's appointments. Monthly newsletters and weekly activity sheets kept everyone informed of planned trips to places like Oklahoma City for horse racing or the theater in Dallas and special events such as the monthly Birthday Blowout (honoring residents with birthdays that month) or visits by various types of entertainers - choral groups from local schools or churches or the nearby air base, for example.

A key selling point was the absence of entry fees. The dining room served three meals a day. A basic monthly rental fee included one meal of your choice each day and additional meals could be added on a daily basis. I loved the place right away. Residents we passed were very friendly and everything was clean and beautifully decorated.

I was especially pleased to note that in the Health Care Center, regardless of their infirmities, most residents were involved in some level of activity rather than sitting alone in their wheelchairs in the halls or propped in front of a TV. One group was having a sing-a-long of old songs and hymns, led by a volunteer and accompanied on piano by a resident from one of the other sections. The lack of odors one traditionally associates with nursing facilities was also encouraging.

At the end of our visit, I put my name on the waiting list for a one bedroom atrium apartment with a walk-in shower. I wasn't really ready to leave my friends in Indianapolis, but was assured that if my name reached the top of the list before I was ready, the open apartment would simply be offered to someone below me and I would remain first in line for future openings.

A Final Indiana Adventure

I returned to Indianapolis and began preparing for my eventual move to Wichita Falls.

Trish's first suspense novel, *Someone to Watch Over*, was due out that fall and the entire family was becoming excited. When I ran across a brochure for the Magna Cum Murder mystery convention at Ball State University in Muncie, I thought it might be fun for Trish and I to attend.

Although we made our plans too late for Trish to join the scheduled panel discussions, we had a wonderful time rubbing elbows with the attending authors and other fans. One author I talked with was Michael Lewin, whose first book we had purchased for the Indiana Division back in 1971.

Two or three tracks of panels with five or six authors on each ran consecutively. The moderators were well chosen and each session allowed time for audience questions. There was much laughter and it was easy to see that authors and fans alike were enjoying themselves. Saturday night's dinner featured an audience participation mystery play that proved just as much fun.

Nancy Pickard, who'd provided a cover quote for Trish's book, was one of the convention's featured authors. Trish was delighted to be able to thank her in person. She was also stunned, when at the beginning of Nancy's next panel, the author began describing the "wonderful new book with an Indiana setting" that she'd recently read.

To say Trish was unprepared when Nancy then introduced her and suggested she stand up and tell everyone about her book would be an understatement. She told me later that her legs were shaking so badly she wasn't sure they would hold her up. Still, once she was on her feet, she managed to give the book's title and reveal that its fictional setting was a small Hoosier town that somewhat resembled Shelbyville.

Nancy had to prompt her to tell everyone when it would be out so they could buy a copy. Trish said the supportive laughter that followed her precise announcement that *Someone to Watch Over* would be on sale, "in nine days," made future public appearances much easier. And, of course, the entire experience also made her a lifetime Nancy Pickard fan.

After listening to such a glowing endorsement of my child's accomplishment, I'm not sure whether it was Trish or me who enjoyed Magna Cum Murder the most.

Sharing a Daughter's Triumph

Knowing that publishers only pay book tour expenses for their best-selling authors, Trish and Jerry organized one on their own. Since the book was set in Indiana, they made fourteen stops in Kansas, Nebraska, Missouri, Illinois, Indiana, and Tennessee and Arkansas before returning to Wichita Falls.

In addition to being chauffeur and head cheerleader, Jerry became quite a good salesman. He wore a cap and T-shirt that advertised the book during every signing and even sold copies to waitresses along their route who asked what had brought them to that particular city.

The day before her scheduled speaking engagement at the Shelbyville library, Trish drove me to get my hair done. Judy, my hairdresser and the other girls in the shop were quite excited about knowing a *real* author and bought several of the books Trish had brought with her. By the time my hair was done, Judy's customers had caught the book buying fever and Trish had sold and signed twenty-two books!

Jeff had flown in from Washington, D.C. to surprise his parents, but that night at a mystery book store in Indianapolis I had a surprise reunion of my own. My old "roommate" from my library acquisition trips, Tom Krasean and his wife dropped by to see how proud I was of my daughter.

Saturday morning before the library signing, we all attended a small luncheon Trish's friend Margaret Ann Huffman gave in her honor at her home in Shelbyville.

Margaret Ann, an award-winning feature writer for *The Shelbyville News* for many years, had done an in-depth interview with Trish about *Someone to Watch Over* for one of the paper's special sections. Her luncheon was lovely, but Trish remembers little of it because she was so nervous.

She'd given several talks since Nancy Pickard had put her on the spot in Muncie, but she still found the thought of speaking to the hometown crowd very intimidating. On top of that, she was certain only her closest friends were going to show up.

Far from being a small crowd, so many attended that the original site of her talk had to be changed from a meeting room to the lobby. There were people on the inside steps and chairs had to be carried up from the children's level and pulled in from study areas within the main floor stacks.

From behind the library's main desk, she gave a talk entitled "A Chip Off the Old Block," explaining how growing up on the block where both her home and the library were located had influenced her as a writer. One anecdote dealt with her first encounter with prejudice.

Although the Shelbyville schools had been integrated quite early, like most places, prejudice still existed. The owner of the movie theater on our block refused to allow Negroes (as African-Americans were then called) to sit in first floor seats. He would, however, sell them tickets in the balcony. Trish decided very quickly that the fact that her best friends, the Hord children, could not sit with her at the movies was unfair.

What made the recounting of the episode so moving was that Rev. Hord had recently returned to the Second Baptist Church and was at the library to hear her speak. Although his wife was ill and he couldn't stay for the signing itself, they had a wonderful reunion before he had to leave.

Also attending were many of Trish's friends from the bank she had worked in for fifteen years before her move to Texas. Schoolmates from both Jerry's and Trish's classes - including one who still lived in Shelbyville but had never attended any of Trish's class reunions - turned out in force as well. And, although Jerry's father had passed away the year before and his mother now lived with his sister in Florida, several other members of his family were there. Many of my old friends also came to the event.

When she finished speaking and fielding questions, Trish moved to the original meeting room and signed books for almost three hours.

I was so proud of her. Everyone wanted to know whether I had suspected she had such talent. I told them I'd gotten a hint when, in the fifth grade, she'd won an American Legion writing contest on "What America Means to Me". I also recounted how she had always made up stories and acted them out with her dolls.

To cap off what had been a very successful but tiring day, several of Jerry and Trish's closest friends joined us for dinner in Indianapolis. The next morning the book tour moved on, Jeff flew back to Washington, and I was left to recuperate from all the excitement.

TWENTY-TWO

WICHITA FALLS

When the marketing director of Rolling Meadows called in March of 1995 to say a one bedroom would soon be available, I felt the time was right to move on.

Until that point, I had not actually told my friends that I was thinking of moving. I had, however, begun to prepare them by talking about how much I wanted to be closer to Trish. Still, it was a shock when I finally revealed my plans.

I knew that finding a buyer for my house might take several weeks or even months, but I'd been reluctant to list the house until I knew I had a permanent place to go. Storing my things and moving in with Trish and Jerry for some unknown period would have required me to make two separate adjustments.

The same evening I signed the listing agreement with Rhoda, the realtor who'd sold Trish and Jerry's home, another agent from her company brought a couple by and asked permission to show the house. Rhoda had mentioned her new listing as he was heading out to my area with his clients and they were eager to see the house.

Next day when I returned from an errand, Rhoda called and said, "The house just sold." It seemed the couple from the previous evening had taken a second look while I was out and met my asking price. The only problem was that they wanted possession as quickly as possible.

In preparation for my move, I'd been going through my possessions and discarding things I would not need or be able to fit into my new home, but it was clear I'd not done enough. My apartment would be seven hundred and twenty-nine square feet. My house was about eleven hundred. Although I'd be eliminating two bedrooms, paring down the trappings of home ownership and the accumulation of many years takes a great deal of time.

Trish flew up about ten days before I would have to vacate and we began filling boxes and disposing of the things. Piece by piece and box by box the rooms began to empty.

We delivered a full car load of books on Indiana history to the nearest library branch. I expected that most of them would wind up in their annual book sale, but when the librarian began to go through them, she kept saying, "We don't have this one. Or these. Oh my, we could use this series. I think we'll be keeping most of what you have here." She made me feel much better about leaving my old book friends behind.

Once I'd broken the news to my friends that I was leaving, they got a group together to say farewell. My friends at the Quaker Guild also organized a farewell party for me and people from the library took me to Sunday dinner at one of our favorite eating places. In addition, Judy, my hairdresser of twenty-three years threw a surprise party for me at her shop.

I'd baked and taken Christmas cookies to twenty people for many years. Each of them mentioned how they'd miss me - and those cookies. At my surprise party Judy gave me the party tablecloth signed by everyone there and also a beautiful craft birdhouse that she'd made. The birdhouse now hangs outside my apartment door to greet my visitors and remind me of home.

Although I told them I would, most of my friends warned me I'd never come back for a visit. But when Trish returned to Magna Cum Murder to promote her second book, *Buried Secrets*, I decided to travel with her but skip the convention and visit my old friends as I'd promised.

I made many wonderful friends during the years I lived and worked in Indianapolis. I'm very happy in my new home, but, oh, how I miss them all.

Moving Day

While Jerry and Trish drove a fully loaded U-Haul truck with its attached trailer for my car (which Jerry was taking as a work vehicle), I flew to Wichita Falls. There I was met by Jeff, who'd traveled from Washington, DC to help me handle the final arrangements at Rolling Meadows.

We had a ready crew of helpers waiting when Jerry and Trish arrived. Jerry and Jeff and Pam's husband Bruce ferried things (via the elevator) to my third-floor apartment. Pam and Trish emptied boxes and I directed (or tried to) where the contents should go. We had additional help in the form of Becca, who at sixteen months investigated every box.

A short time after we began moving things in, my neighbors from either side of my apartment came over to introduce themselves and welcome me to Rolling Meadows. It gave me a warm feeling and made me feel right at home.

I was happy to finally be closer to my family, but by this time I was very tired. So after everyone left, I fixed my first meal in my new kitchen and crawled into bed.

And so, on April 10, 1995, I began a new phrase of my life, in Wichita Falls, Texas. I had come a long way and experienced many things since my birth as a country doctor's youngest daughter in the small town of Homer, Indiana.

A Texas Welcome

Before I went to sleep that first night, I read the resident's manual which mentioned that in case of a fire an alarm bell would ring. At three A.M. that night I awakened to the most awful ringing and immediately jumped out of bed.

I wasn't really awake yet and thought the racket must be coming from the boxes that I had piled up. After pawing through them, I realized what it must be and opened my door. Outside on that same wall a bell was ringing and a light was flashing. I quickly shut the door and tried to remember what I was supposed to do. Then I realized I was to go out on my balcony.

I rushed out expecting to see kindred souls out on other balconies, but there I stood all alone. Just then the alarm quit, so I went back to bed. The next morning I told the marketing director that I appreciated the loud welcome to Texas, but did they really have to schedule it for three o'clock in the morning?

Making Friends and Keeping Busy

As with most social situations, people tend to settle into groups with common interests. The dining tables at Rolling Meadows are no exception, however, someone is always absent for one reason or other, leaving an open spot.

During my first few days, different people had openings and invited me to join them. Then I became friends with Necie Prystas and began sharing her table. Necie's sense of humor was much like mine and we both loved to read and traded books. She introduced me to the group who played spinner dominos and I began joining them every evening. Christine Gay was also a very good friend of Necie's and mine. The three of us started going everywhere together and calling ourselves the three Musketeers.

Dominos is just one of my regular activities. On Monday nights we play quarter bingo. Once a month we have a Birthday Blowout honoring residents with birthday that month. Each one has a different theme and features a special menu and entertainment such as western night with ranch style food and a cowboy singer or a prime rib dinner that featured a mystery play.

Also once a month is a men's breakfast, and on another day a Gourmet Getaway takes those who sign up to different restaurants in Wichita Falls or one of the area's small towns for lunch.

Soon after I settled in, we started an exercise class three mornings a week. Along with the exercises, we've learned line dancing and the Macarena. During the winter we concentrate on aerobics or Tai Chi. In the summer, we add evening sessions of water aerobics in the heated outside pool. We old folks aren't the only ones who love that pool. Whenever Pam brings Becca up from Austin to visit, she wants to go to Mam-ma's to swim.

Apartments are cleaned twice a month; so outside of picking up trash and a little in-between dusting, housekeeping is simple. Laundry facilities are available in each building, or for a fee, that chore can also be eliminated.

I know most people hate the thought of being forced into a retirement home, but the cottages and apartments here are like private homes or condos and the help offered as you grow older makes it a very desirable place. Of course, I've always been a practical person. I chose to move here of my own volition, before that choice was taken from me.

But I've never regretted giving up my home and moving closer to my family. I enjoy almost every minute and, although I have a few problems, they would be much worse if I'd remained at home alone, stubbornly clinging to the material pieces of a life I could no longer handle by myself.

Everything Has a Downside

Because of allergies to several medicines and foods, I do find that meals can be a problem. Long before I moved I developed allergies to fish and seafood and any form of peppers. Fish is easy to avoid, but unfortunately, Texas wouldn't be Texas without Mexican food. Thus, it often becomes a challenge on any given day to identify which foods are pepper-free. Just a tiny piece or two of bell pepper or pimento used to flavor or garnish a vegetable or entree can result in severe itching or hives.

Fish on Friday isn't a hardship unless the other entree is stuffed green peppers (which I used to love) or meat cooked with peppers. Thankfully, I can always order a sandwich, baked potato or French fries and the salad bar is outstanding so I get along just fine.

My most pressing problem is the progressive eye disease, macular degeneration. I see an ophthalmologist regularly, but reading regular print is almost impossible and recently, even large print books have become a chore. The Texas library system offers a talking books program for those with impaired vision, so their tapes now keep me connected to the world of books.

Now my memory is something else. I find I forget names and words. This affliction has grown worse in recent months. While I try to substitute other words for the one I want to use, this can sure hamper the sense of the sentence. Still, I do better than many others around me.

Facing Life With Humor

I've always believed the ability to laugh at your own foibles helps keep you going longer. With that in mind, I'm going to share some of the stories about my fellow residents. I in no way mean to make fun of my friends or anyone else. But younger generations would do much better if they could understood how the process of aging affects those they loved. And how it will almost certainly eventually affect them.

When new people come in to Rolling Meadows they're usually in relatively fair health. But as the years go by they begin to deteriorate. I've lost Necie to cancer and Christine Gay to heart failure and Mac and Aunt Bea (spinner partners) to diabetes. Aunt Bea was ninety-seven, but her mind was sharp until her death.

Shortly before Necie's death, Juanita Martin moved into one of the cottages and joined us at our lunch table. With Necie and Christine gone, Juanita has now become my closest friend.

Several residents who were here when I came are in different stages of Alzheimers. In theory, the families of residents with this affliction must find a specialized home for their loved ones when the symptoms of the disease begin to bother others. In reality, there's a long waiting list for such care facilities.

Mitch once owned a children's clothing and shoe store and often told stories of how he helped poor families during the depression. He liked bright colors and complemented anyone who wore them. He called the men old buzzards and, if they were balding, told them to stop copying his hair style. If a man was playing spinner dominos with two ladies, he'd pretend to be jealous. He'd gone to college in Oklahoma where he played horn in the band and often played music he remembered on the piano.

Despite having Alzheimers, for a long time he was a perfect gentlemen, able to function with assistance. He loved to dance and usually helped people on and off the bus whenever we went anywhere. But his constant repetition of the same questions almost drove us to distraction. Eventually, his family moved him to a care facility that was closer to his son's home in Dallas.

Jeanette often didn't know where she was nor what she was supposed to be doing. Yet she was still able to play dominos, add up the score, recite song lyrics and perform a little dance. Just as Mitch could recite long poems he'd learned in school.

Then there was Cloma who'd had a tumor removed from her brain and could not keep track of her purse. It was more like a satchel really and held everything under the sun, even a box of dominos. It weighed a ton. She eventually became very ill and now resides in health care.

Bertha who's alert most of the time, spent her first year here crying because she'd just lost her husband. Finally a niece took her in hand and made her cut her hair and wear something other than the suit her husband had liked. Bertha still loses her jacket or her keys and forgets what she's planned to do and, like Jeanette, who fell asleep on a couch in the atrium, often dozes off in the activity room.

I found it interesting that several of those who were suffering from Alzheimers or other mental troubles gravitated together. Jeanette and Mitch and Cloma and Bertha played dominos together every night for several years. Cloma kept score and furnished the dominos from her oversized purse. She and Mitch became especially close, which was sad in a way. The little group was broken up when Cloma's tumor returned and she moved to the health care section.

Mitch was so lost without her. He wandered around trying to find her, but as his disease progressed, he often couldn't remember her name and would ask where "that other lady" was. Bertha knew she was in health care and led the others over to visit her. After that, Mitch began showing up in Cloma's room early in the morning and interrupting her bath and was soon forbidden to visit at all.

I do not look forward to any of these things happening to me, but I'm aware that someday they might. With that in mind, and remembering how exhausting caring for my own mother was, I've instructed Trish and her children that they are not to feel guilty about moving me to whatever facility can care for me best if I become unable to live even with assistance. All I've asked is that the place be clean and well run.

One Last Hold on Independence

Even though living in a retirement complex eliminates worries such as safety, cleaning and home maintenance, and transportation, the responsibility for personal finances must be addressed.

Until she herself became ill again, Cloma took care of Jeanette's daily needs by helping her dress and keeping track of her appointments. But Jeanette had a nephew by marriage who took care of her business affairs. He and his wife would come and play dominos after they had eaten dinner with her.

Cloma had children and grandchildren who visited her often. One grandchild would sometimes stay overnight with her and play bingo and other games. The whole family was involved in church activities. Their minister often gave the message at chapel and the children sang and played guitar. They were a nice family.

So far, with only minor help from Trish, I remain able to handle my own finances and appointment schedule. As my eyes deteriorate further, I know this will have to change. But I remember how quickly Mother went downhill after Doc insisted that she transfer the responsibility for the farms to a manager and am trying to hold out as long as possible.

I truly believe that challenging your mind - be it through games like dominos or Yahtzee® or cards - will keep you sharp far longer than will staring at a TV all day or crying for hours about what can't be changed.

I also believe in facing reality. Since I have no desire to live out my final days as a mindless vegetable, I've executed a living will and a "do not resuscitate" order is part of my medical file. Trish is aware of my wishes and I trust her to carry them out. With her help I've also planned my funeral service and prepaid those expenses.

That said, it's important to know that those of us who are aging never miss a chance to celebrate life. Mable Hampton recently had a 100th birthday party. Although the residents were invited, I was visiting the grandchildren in Austin and missed the celebration. I'm told her family organized a beautiful party.

Marjory Holsey's son from Georgia sent letters to her friends asking them to write about their friendship with her. He sent pages that fit into a notebook and included an addressed and stamped envelope. Then he flew her to Georgia for the birthday party and presented her with two notebooks filled with the story of her life and pictures from her babyhood to the present.

Fortunately, becoming ill does not always mean death for someone who's aging. Marjorie Neale became very ill with pneumonia and other problems and was transferred to the health care unit. When her daughter wheeled her over to see us, Marjorie was completely out of it. I really thought she had only a week or so to live. Then they discovered that her real problem was her medication and insufficient nourishment. Now she flits around like a sixty-year-old and is exercising with us, going on the Gourmet Getaways, and to the grocery store every week.

The True Test of Love

Ed is very quiet and shy. His wife Mai Tom had a stroke and is in Health Care because she can neither talk nor use her hands. He brings her to his apartment at least once a day where they watch old movies. If she is not well enough to visit him, he goes to sit by her bed.

Such devotion is not uncommon in our generation. Ed showed us some pictures of the two of them when they were young. She was beautiful and he was a handsome fellow. He ran a grocery business near Dallas after serving in World War II. Mai Tom worked in a photography shop. He misses not being able to play golf, but enjoys the putting green at Rolling Meadows.

Bill, an ex-Army officer, recently lost his wife but now has a girlfriend named Pat at Presbyterian Manor (another retirement complex in Wichita Falls). They like traveling together and recently took a trip on the Delta Queen. Bill picks her up for the Gourmet Getaways and often brings her to bingo on Mondays.

Some of the residents thought six months was too soon for Bill to begin dating. But I remember what Rev. Horner once told me. He said, "A woman can always manage without a man. But a man is lost without his wife to guide him. If anything ever happened to my sweet Emma, I expect I'd marry within six months. I would need that help and guidance. It would be a tribute to show how much I loved Emma and could not do without her."

Some of us who play spinner dominos often remain in the activities room after the games to just talk. Our topics vary, but our chats are always stimulating and fun. Trish refers to these sessions as "faculty" meetings - those of us who still have them always attend.

I sometimes wonder if someone at Rolling Meadows will be writing their own memoirs in a few years and tell tales about "that crazy Macdonald woman who used to live here"?

REFLECTIONS

My father taught me many things as I was growing up: Be strong. Tell the truth. Admit your mistakes and forgive those of others. Have compassion and sympathy for those less fortunate. Love one another. And above all, have faith in God.

As the remaining days of my life grow shorter, I begin to think more and more of the past. Sometimes that long ago visit to the gypsy fortune teller comes to mind.

When she read my palm, the gypsy predicted that the letter M would play an important part in my life. She said, "Your career will start in Michigan. You will also marry a man whose name begins with the letter M and have two children." Then she noted my heart line was very short, but my life line was very long.

My career as a librarian began at Michigan State and my husband's name was Macdonald. I lost one child, then gave birth to a second. Colin died only five years after we were married, confirming that my heart line was very short. And now here I am -- living to be an old, old lady as my life line predicted.

I haven't had an episode of premonition in many years. Nor have I been plagued by precognitive nightmares. But then my life is fairly stress-free these days. Whether or not I receive warning of the final event in my life isn't really important.

What matters is that I've lived a pretty good life. I was raised in a caring family by a man with gentle wisdom and a remarkable woman. I loved and was loved by a wonderful man. I bore a daughter whose own life brought me a surrogate son and two beautiful grandchildren. And I know that life will go on in the form of my smart and funny great-granddaughter, RaBecca.

All in all, it's been an interesting journey for a country doctor's youngest daughter.

A DAUGHTER'S ADDENDUM

My husband Jerry Skillman retired in October of 1999. Our daughter Pamela, who now lived in the Austin, Texas area, had separated from her husband and was raising our granddaughter RaBecca (Becca) as a single mother. Son Jeffrey and his partner, Jay Velgos, had also relocated to Austin, a long, five hour drive from Wichita Falls, Texas.

When we began planning our move to be closer to both families, Mother agreed that she needed to make the move as well. Rolling Meadows had been a perfect setting for her, but at 88, her declining health and eyesight issues meant an eventual move from her apartment to the facility's assisted living wing.

Our move was taking us to New Braunfels, a Texas hill country town about 40 miles from Austin. Finding a comparable complex in that area proved too costly. At last we settled on Redwood Springs Assisted Living in San Marcos, a twenty-five minute drive from our new location.

As she had numerous times in the past, Mother soon settled in and made new friends. Her mind remained sharp but her health continued to decline. The following spring she lost a kidney to cancer but kept on going. My grandfather's teachings and philosophy sustained her as it had for the previous 90 years.

She still listened to Books on Tape from the Texas State Library and tried to join in with the facility's activities but life became a series of doctor and hospital visits. The son-in-law she embraced as the son she and my father might have had if fate had allowed, drove her everywhere, loading walkers and eventually a wheelchair into our trunk with no complaints.

Eventually, we realized Redwood Springs wasn't the best fit for her condition and she moved yet again, this time to Sterling House Assisted Living in New Braunfels, only twelve minutes from our house. By then she was in a wheelchair much of the time.

The staff was very good to her and allowed her to remain in her own apartment when it came time for the local Hospice to step in.

Shortly before Mother's 95 birthday, the Shelbyville Library where I had spent so much of my childhood devouring the mystery and suspense novels that laid the groundwork for the books I eventually wrote, purchased Grandmother Barnett's old home. To our delight, they relocated their genealogy department into the space. We were even more pleased when I was asked by the local paper to submit a piece about growing up in the little house behind the library.

A Final Celebration

We all believed Mother had been holding on to reach her milestone 95th birthday on July 25, 2006. Our celebration consisted of cake and ice cream in the facility's sunroom. Jerry and I, Pamela and Becca, and Jeffrey and Jay made sure there was lots of laughter and reminiscing and an abundance of hugs. Mother even managed to join in a quick game of Yahtzee®. I read to her the completed text of the article that was to be published in the Shelbyille News in a week or so. Then Jeffrey wheeled her back to her apartment and we all headed home.

Sixteen days later, on August 10, 2006, Pamela and I were by Mother's side when she passed. When I phoned my husband at his part-time retirement job, he cried even harder than I did.

On August 15, the Shelbyville News ran the article "Genealogy House Roots" along with two photos I had sent with the draft. One was of Mother and me, taken at the 95th birthday party. The other was a 1950s era snapshot of Mother fixing hot dogs for me, my date and another couple shortly after 1:00 a.m. on the morning of New Year's Day. Her electrifying smile in that one could have powered our entire block.

An Editor's comment at the end of the article noted Mother's death and a brief notice on the obituary page echoed that same information. A copy of the text of her full obituary that followed a few days later appears after this update.

An Unexpected Visitor and Echoes of the Past

Mother's well-planned funeral service was not to be. She'd outlived every direct member of her family line and most of her old friends were also gone.

Rev. Horner, the last pastor she worked for as secretary of the First Christian Church, was suffering from Alzheimers. She'd been aware of this for some time and had agreed to let us redo her plans into a Celebration of Life to be held in the parlor of the East Hill Mausoleum in Rushville, Indiana where my father and her parents were interred.

Jeffrey and Jay downloaded the songs she'd requested and we all combed through albums and boxes of old photos that the boys spun into a repeating loop on a laptop computer. The music, which would play softly while we greeted any visitors, began and ended with my parents' song, the haunting melody of Hoagy Carmichael's "Stardust".

We didn't expect a crowd but were pleased to be able to share memories of Mother's life with about a dozen people.

Martha, the youngest and only surviving member of Mother's library quartet known affectionately as "The Girls", had enlisted a former colleague who also knew Mother to make the drive from Indianapolis. The daughter and son-in-law of one of the deceased "Girls" also joined us, as did two of our children's teachers, my best friend and her husband and Jerry's cousin and his wife.

One elderly visitor who didn't even know Mother offered us a poignant touch of closure.

Hugh Mull introduced himself as the president of the mausoleum board, then said he couldn't stay for the service, but simply wanted to pay his respects to the last of Dr. Barnett's children. It seems my grandfather had saved his life at age four during a diphtheria epidemic, a disease I knew all too well.

I read a few excerpts from these memoirs. Pamela and Jeffrey shared funny and heartfelt stories of their travels and visits with their grandmother. Jeffrey triggered the final song on

Mother's play list, The Lord's Prayer, not sung by Rev. Horner as she'd planned, but a nice version we hoped she'd have liked.

And then we were done. Or so we thought.

Mother and Daddy were together again and we had enough memories to last our own lifetimes. But knowing Mother's history of premonitions I truly believe she somehow orchestrated the final touch to the day.

Our family habit after an anniversary or funeral or similar gathering was to have lunch or dinner at The Kopper Kettle Inn, an historic restaurant housed in a 150+ year old way station in Morristown, Indiana. The surroundings match the age of the building, the waitresses wear period costumes and the family-style fried chicken dinners and sugar cream pie will banish any clouds of sadness diners might harbor.

As we were being led to our reserved table Jeffrey grabbed my arm and whispered, "Listen."

The soundtrack of the music playing softly in the background was "Stardust." Jeffrey was grinning ear to ear.

"I guess Mom was happy with our celebration," I murmured as we joined the rest of the family and prepared to continue our lives without the country doctor's youngest daughter.

Frances Macdonald

Frances Barnett Macdonald, 95, of New Braunfels, Texas, died Thursday, August 10 at her home.

Born July 25, 1911, in Homer, she was the daughter of Dr. Daniel E. and Cora (McGinnis) Barnett. She married Colin C. Macdonald married on Oct. 18, 1941, in East Lansing, Mich., and he preceded her in death on Jan. 6, 1946.

Survivors include one daughter Patricia "Trish" (husband Jerry) Skillman of New Braunfels; two grandchildren, Pamela Bartee of Elgin, Texas, and Jeffrey Skillman (partner, Jay Velgos) of Austin, Texas; great-granddaughter RaBecca Bartee of Elgin; and several nieces and nephews.

She also was preceded in death by her parents, two sisters and one brother, Arthur R Barnett.

Mrs. Macdonald was a former Shelbyville resident.

She had been employed at the Michigan State University Library from 1937 to 1941 and as a manuscript librarian for the Indiana State Library from 1962 to 1974, and retired as head of their Indiana Division in 1978.

Mrs. Macdonald graduated in 1929 from Shelbyville High School, where she was editor of the yearbook, Squib. She received her bachelor of arts degree from the University of Michigan and her bachelor of science degree from Case Western Reserve University.

She was a member of the First Christian Church of Shelbyville, where she served as secretary-treasure and board member; Indiana Historical Society; Indianapolis Museum of Art; the Woodruff chapter of the International Travel Study Club; and Alpha Xi Delta sorority.

A memorial celebration will be 10:30 a.m. at the East Hill Shrine Mausoleum, 779 E. State Road 44 in Rushville.

Right: Frances Macdonald and Santa, Christmas 2000, at Redwood Springs Assisted Living in San Marcos, TX

Below: "The Three Musketeers," Christine Gay, Niecie Prystas, and Frances Macdonald

Below, clockwise: Pam and RaBecca Bartee; Jerry and Trish Skillman; Jeffrey Skillman; and Frances Macdonald on her 95th birthday

Jerry and Trish Skillman's 50th Anniversary,
November 5, 2010, in Kauai, HI

Frances Macdonald's great-granddaughter RaBecca Michelle Bartee and
granddaughter Pamela Bartee,
December 2012

Frances Macdonald's grandson
Jeffrey Skillman and Jay Velgos on
their wedding day, June 6, 2014 in
Hilo, HI

01/09/1773 George D. Barnett (my paternal great-great-grandfather) is born

11/04/1782 Delilah Davis (my paternal great-great-great-grandmother is born

11/01/1793 James W. Walker (my maternal great-great-great-grandfather) is born

10/13/1796 Margaret U. (Wood) Walker (my maternal great-great-great-grandmother) is born

??/??/1800 Sally Yarnell (my paternal great-grandmother is born

08/09/1802 William McGinnis is born (my maternal great-grandfather)

05/12/1803 James D. Barnett (my paternal great-grandfather is born

10/18/1807 Sarah Harbour is born (my maternal great-grandmother)

08/29/1826 Lemuel Hoak (my maternal great-grandfather) is born in Champaign County, Ohio

10/12/1826 Lucretia Walker (may maternal great-grandmother) is born

02/08/1831 William McGinnis marries Sarah Harbour

11/27/1832 James D. Barnett marries Sally Yarnell in Vermilion, IL

??/??/1841 Robert Edward Barnett is born (my paternal grandfather)

02/14/1842 George D. Barnett dies in Indianaola, IL

11/12/1843 James W. Walker dies.

11/08/1845 Lewis Abner McGinnis (my maternal grandfather) is born to William and Sarah (Harbour) McGinnis

11/14/1845 Delilah (Davis) Barnett dies in Indianaola, IL

11/26/1846 Lemuel Hoak marries Lucreia Walker

??/??/1848 Sally (Yarnell) Barnett dies

08/27/1849 Lavenia Hoak (my maternal grandmother) is born in Ohio

07/08/1854 Mary Elizabeth Martin is born (my paternal grand-mother)

03/27/1862 Lewis Abner McGinnis enlists at age 16 in Co. A, 61st Regiment Inf. Vol. at Camp Chase (61st and 82nd Ohio later combined as 82nd Regiment)

12/30/1866 James D. Barnett dies

09/13/1870 Lewis Abner McGinnis marries Lavenia Hoak

??/??/1870 Robert Edward Barnett marries Mary Elizabeth Martin

05/10/1875 Daniel Emmett Barnett (my father) is born in Indianola, IL to Robert Edward and Mary Elizabeth (Martin) Barnett (After Robert's death, Mary Elizabeth married a Miller)

08/21/1877 Cora Lucretia McGinnis (my mother) is born in Fairmount, IL to Lewis Abner and Lavenia (Hoak) McGinnis

07/08/1896 Robert Edward Barnett (my grand-father) dies in ??, IL

06/12/1901 Daniel Emmett Barnett marries Cora Lucretia McGinnis in Sidell, IL (my parents)

08/10/1902 Inez Love Barnett is born in Ann Arbor, MI (my sister)

02/19/1904 Irma Lowene Barnett is born in Ann Arbor, MI (my sister)

11/05/1906 Arthur R. Barnett is born in New Hartford, MO (my brother Doc)

04/18/1909 Lucretia (Walker) Hoak dies

05/10/1910 Lemual Hoak dies in Champaign County, Ohio

06/26/1911 Colin Campbell Macdonald (my husband) is born to Edward Albert and Ruth (Woodward) Macdonald in Detroit, MI

07/25/1911 Frances Marie Barnett (me) is born in Homer, IN

06/22/1926 Lavenia (Hoak) McGinnis dies

08/22/1927 Inez Love Barnett marries Gifford Upjohn

11/17/1928	Harold Upjohn (my nephew) is born to Love and Gifford Upjohn
05/31/1929	Frances Marie Barnett graduates from Shelbyville High School, Shelbyville, IN
12/28/1931	Nancy Upjohn (my niece) is born to Love and Gifford Upjohn
05/26/1932	Lewis Abner McGinnis dies in Audubon, Iowa
08/17/1940	Arthur R. (Doc) Barnett marries Hanne K. Beck in Lafayette, IN
06/18/1941	Charles Barnett (my nephew) is born to Arthur R. (Doc) and Hanne Barnett
10/18/1941	Frances Marie Barnett marries Colin Campbell Macdonald in East Lansing, MI
08/21/1942	Colin Campbell Macdonald enlists in Army Air Force as a 2nd Lt.
11/18/1942	Dr. Daniel Emmett Barnett (my father) dies in Homer, IN
04/04/1943	Patricia Macdonald (my daughter) is born to Colin Campbell and Frances Marie (Barnett) Macdonald in Shelbyville, IN
12/29/1944	Daniel Barnett (my nephew) is born to Arthur R. (Doc) and Hanne Barnett
12/30/1944	Irma Lowene Barnett is married to Cyril Joseph Wittliff in Detroit, MI
01/06/1946	Colin Campbell Macdonald (my husband) dies in Fitzsimmons Hospital in Denver, CO
11/05/1960	Patricia Macdonald marries Jerry Homer Skillman in Shelbyville, IN
03/28/1961	Cora Lucretia (McGinnis) Barnett (my mother) dies in Shelbyville, IN
06/09/1961	Pamela Michelle Skillman (my granddaughter) is born in Shelbyville, IN
08/29/1963	Jeffrey Hale Skillman (my grandson) is born in Shelbyville, IN
08/??/1985	Irma Lowene (Barnett) Wittliff dies in Mesa, AZ
02/11/1987	Arthur Barnett dies in Shelbyville, IN

08/14/1987   Inez Love (Barnett) Upjohn dies in Kalamazoo, MI

09/14/1991   Pamela Michelle Skillman marries Bruce Hudson Bartee in Wichita Falls, TX

12/21/1993   RaBecca Michelle Bartee (my great-granddaughter) is born in Austin, TX

09/28/2000   Pamela Skillman Bartee and Bruce Bartee are divorced in Austin, TX

08/10/2006   Frances Marie Barnett Macdonald dies in New Braunfels, TX

06/06/2014   Jeffrey Hale Skillman is legally married to Jay Velgos, his partner of 20+ years, on the Big Island of Hawaii. Somewhere the country doctor's youngest daughter would have been smiling that the event she'd long hoped for had finally been able to take place.

03/12/2016   Jay Velgos dies in Austin, TX